EDITOR: LEE JOHNSON

MEN-AT-ARMS

IMPERIAL CHINESE ARMIES (2) 590-1260 AD

Text by
CHRIS PEERS
Colour plates by
MICHAEL PERRY

First published in Great Britain in 1996 by Osprey, an
imprint of Reed Consumer Books Ltd., Michelin House,
81 Fulham Road,
London SW3 6RB
and Auckland, Melbourne, Singapore and Toronto
© Copyright 1996 Reed International Books Ltd.

ISBN 1 85532 599 3

Filmset in Great Britain by KDI, Newton le Willows
Printed through World Print Ltd, Hong Kong

Acknowledgements
The author would especially like to thank the following for
their help and encouragement: Duncan Head, Thom
Richardson of the Royal Armouries, HM Tower of London,
and the staff of the Department of Oriental Antiquities at the
British Museum.

Publisher's note
Readers may wish to consult this book in conjunction with
the following Osprey publications:

MAA 25 Medieval Chinese Armies 1260–1520 AD
MAA 218 *Ancient Chinese Armies*
MAA 284 *Imperial Chinese Armies (1) 200 BC–589 AD*

Artist's note
Readers may care to note that the original paintings from
which the colour plates in this book were prepared are available for private sale. All reproduction copyright whatsoever is
retained by the Publisher. All enquiries should be addressed
to:

Michael Perry,
3 Quorn Close,
Attenborough,
Nottingham NG9 6BU

The Publishers regret that they can enter into no correspon-
dence upon this matter.

IMPERIAL CHINESE ARMIES (2) FROM THE SUI TO THE SUNG 590–1260 AD

INTRODUCTION

By AD 589, when Yang Chien established himself at the head of a newly reunified Chinese empire, nearly four centuries had elapsed since the fall of the last great imperial dynasty: the Han. Although Yang's new Sui regime consciously modelled itself on its great predecessor, both China and the world outside had changed. While the Han, like their own ancestors, the Chou, had with some justification regarded their empire as an island of civilisation surrounded by uncouth 'barbarians', by Sui and T'ang times this concept no longer bore any relation to the real world. Huge Turkish and Tibetan empires had imposed a measure of central control over Central Asia, through which flowed trade and pilgrimage routes extending from Korea to the Mediterranean. Literacy, city life and centralised governments were no longer restricted to a few privileged enclaves, but were rapidly spreading across the whole Eurasian continent – a process largely complete by the end of the 8th century. The problem for the Sui and their successors was no longer simply to 'overawe the barbarians', but to deal as equals with other cultures that were just as proud and self-confident as their own.

China's ultimate failure to come to terms with this situation is well known, but in the period under discussion here, the empire was probably more receptive to outside influences than ever before or since. Turkish cavalry techniques contributed to the effectiveness of the T'ang armies that in the mid-7th century advanced China's frontiers to their greatest pre-modern extent. Political and commercial relations flourished with peoples as far afield as Iraq and Java, and Christian, Jewish and Muslim traders established colonies throughout the country. Eventually, beginning in the 10th century, these factors fused to produce what has often been described by historians as an economic and technological revolution.

The recurring political pattern of Chinese history, with its cycle of unifications, dynastic declines and eventual reunifications, has sometimes given observers the impression that its civilisation as a whole was static, but nothing could be further from the truth. The Sung period's booming cash economy, its social mobility and its technical achievements made it not only very different from the T'ang, but in many ways more 'modern' than any other society on earth at the time. This trend influenced the conduct of warfare in two ways: it encouraged the development of weapons

Figures representing heavy cavalry on armoured horses are common in 6th- and 7th-century tombs. This example, dating from the Sui or early T'ang period, is wearing a variant of the popular 'cord and plaque' armour (see the reconstruction in Plate A). (By courtesy of the Trustees of the British Museum)

such as gunpowder, which, spreading from China to the outside world in the 13th century, was to make possible the European conquest of most of the world; but it also encouraged the demilitarisation of Chinese society – already favoured by Confucian idealists – as new ways arose for people of all classes to achieve status and wealth.

The period covered here was perhaps as significant as any in the history of China's armed forces. At its beginning the Sui and T'ang armies, fighting with bow and spear and led by hereditary, half-barbarian warrior clans, were clearly the heirs of ancient Chinese and Central Asian traditions. By its conclusion the Sung, with their long-service professional soldiers backed up by mass-produced explosive weapons, seem to point the way towards the modern world.

Sources for the Sui and T'ang are not dissimilar to those for earlier periods. The tradition, begun under the Han, of producing an official history based on the court documents of each dynasty continued: the T'ang, in fact, has two such histories, the *Chiu T'ang Shu* and the *Hsin T'ang Shu*. The surviving work of Ssu-ma Kuang, a Sung dynasty scholar, also provides a narrative based on these and other, now lost, sources. Then there are other valuable works, such as Wen Ta-ya's eyewitness *Ta-T'ang Ch'uang-yeh Ch'i-chu Chu*, or 'Diary of the Founding of the Great T'ang', which corrects some of the bias of the official accounts, and the mainly religious documents excavated at Tun-huang. By Sung times these unofficial sources are much more extensive, and include regional histories as well as a series of extant military encyclopaedias.

The chronicles mentioned above are supplemented by abundant archaeological material; although few pieces of armour or weaponry have survived, tomb figurines and paintings help to fill in many gaps in our knowledge. The Sung period was perhaps the 'golden age' of Chinese painting, and while military subjects were not particularly popular, where they do occur they are treated with unprecedented realism and attention to detail. Especially noteworthy are the numerous wall paintings and statues from Tun-huang, in the far north-west of China. Although they deal mainly with Buddhist religious subjects, there is plenty of material of use to the military historian.

CHRONOLOGY

589 Reunification of China completed by Yang Chien.

612-614 Sui campaigns against Koguryo in Korea.

618 Yang-ti assassinated. Collapse of Sui dynasty.

623 Central government restored under T'ang dynasty.

630-648 T'ang conquest of the Tarim Basin.

661-665 T'ang protectorate over the Western Turks.

660-668 New war in Korea.

c.670 Tibetans overrun Tarim Basin.

690-705 Interregnum under the Chou dynasty of Empress Wu.

736-755 War with Tibet. T'ang authority established briefly as far west as the Pamirs.

751-752 T'ang armies defeated on three fronts by Nan-chao, Arabs and Khitans.

755-763 Rebellion of An Lu-shan.

808 Sha-to Turks settle in north-west China.

875-884 Rebellion of Huang Ch'ao.

907 Last T'ang Emperor deposed by Chu Wen. Khitans found Liao dynasty in Manchuria.

c.920 Naphtha bombs and flamethrowers in use in south China.

936 Liao occupy north-east China.

960 Chao K'uang-yin establishes Sung dynasty.

1004-1119 Wars between Sung and Tanguts in the north-west.

1038 Yuan-hao proclaims Tangut Western Hsia dynasty.

1044 First mention of gunpowder in a Sung military manual.

1068-1086 Unsuccessful military reforms of Wang An-shih.

c.1125 Metal-cased explosive bombs developed.

1125 Liao dynasty overthrown by Jurchen.

1127 Fall of K'aifeng to Jurchen. Establishment of Kin dynasty. Sung retreat to Lin-an in the south – the 'Southern Sung'.

1161 Major Kin invasion defeated by Sung navy.

1227 Fall of Western Hsia to Mongols.

1235 Kin dynasty destroyed by Mongols.

1260 Foundation of Mongol Yuan dynasty by Kubilai Khan. Beginning of final campaign against the Sung.

THE SUI DYNASTY, AD 589–618

Yang Chien, who became the emperor Wen-ti, the first ruler of the Sui, had enjoyed a distinguished military career before he came to the throne, having served under the famous minister of the Western Wei, Yu-wen T'ai. Like most of those who founded dynasties, he was a member of an old aristocratic family, and traced his descent both from the native Chinese gentry and the Hsien-pi tribal chiefs who had migrated from the north-east some three centuries previously.

Yang Chien's conquest in 589 of the last rival Chinese state, Ch'en, did not bring lasting peace to the empire. He at first attempted to conciliate the independent-minded southerners, but his

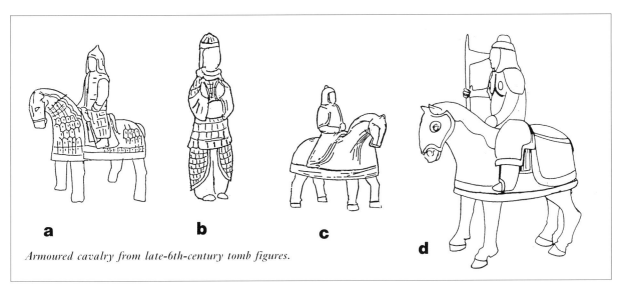

a   **b**   **c**   **d**

Armoured cavalry from late-6th-century tomb figures.

destruction of their old capital at Chien-k'ang sparked rumours that the entire population was to be deported to the north-west. Scattered revolts broke out, and the emperor reverted to his natural authoritarian style, ordering generals Yang Su and P'ei Chu to bring the south to heel – a task which they carried out with great ruthlessness. Furthermore, the loyalty of the people was soon being strained by the enormous public works – including the Grand Canal complex and the rebuilding of thousands of miles of walls in the north-west – which were undertaken using forced labour. Fear of further trouble led to a decree of 590 effectively placing the military outside the capital under the control of local civil officials, and in 595 to the confiscation of privately held weapons. In 598 there was even an attempt to ban all boats over a certain length from the rivers of the south, in order to prevent them from being used to aid rebellion.

In foreign relations, just as at home, Wen-ti was guided by a desire to emulate the achievements of the Han. Like their predecessors, the Sui were faced with a threat from the northern steppes, where the T'u-chueh or eastern Turks – heirs to part of the Turkish Empire which in the mid-6th century had briefly controlled the whole of Central Asia – remained powerful despite serious internal divisions. Wen-ti's policy was to exploit these divisions by supporting rival Turkish factions, and in this way he managed to stave off several potential crises without resorting to all-out warfare. In the south, Chiao-chou (in what is now northern Vietnam) had escaped from Chinese control in the 4th century. An army under Liu Fang reconquered it in 602, but an attempt to advance further south into the kingdom of Champa was less successful. Liu sacked the Champa capital and returned with some valuable loot, but his army was severely weakened by disease on its way home. The court soon lost its enthusiasm for such expeditions, and Champa retained its independence.

Yang-ti, who succeeded to the Sui throne in 604, was even more ambitious. In 607 he led an army to the far west, receiving the submission of the T'u-chueh as well as the kings of Turfan and Hami, while his general Yu-wen Shu inflicted a

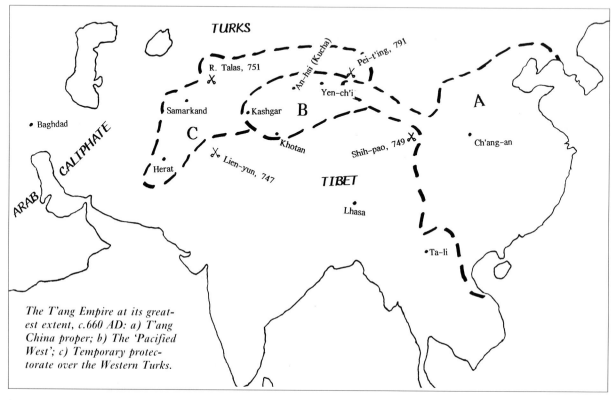

The T'ang Empire at its greatest extent, c.660 AD: a) T'ang China proper; b) The 'Pacified West'; c) Temporary protectorate over the Western Turks.

major defeat on the T'u-yu-hun in the Tarim Basin. At the T'u-chueh court, however, the triumphant emperor made a disturbing discovery: an ambassador from Koguryo, an independent kingdom in northern Korea, was already in residence. Alarmed at the thought of an alliance between these two potentially hostile powers, Yang-ti sent emissaries to Koguryo to demand its formal submission. When this was refused, he began to prepare for war.

This was to be one of the most ambitious campaigns ever undertaken by a Chinese dynasty, using all the resources of a newly unified and self-confident empire. First, a northern branch of the Grand Canal had to be completed to enable supplies to be brought to the frontier from as far away as the Yangtze valley; then a huge army – said to number a million men – was raised. All this, however, was to prove too much for a state not yet fully recovered from centuries of disunity and civil strife.

It was not until 612 that the emperor was able to lead his army across the Liao river on a specially built bridge and into Koguryo. The Koreans, however, were aware of the defensive advantages provided by their terrain and climate, and made the most of them. On the far side of the Liao the Chinese found forested mountains, the few routes through which were blocked by a chain of fortified towns. These resisted throughout the summer, and in the autumn, rains forced Yang-ti to retreat. In 613 he tried again, but a revolt at home obliged him to detach troops to suppress it, and his weakened army was no more successful than it had been the previous year. The following summer he pushed across the Liao yet again, bypassing the fortresses and reaching the capital city of P'yong-yang, but few supplies could get through and the troops began to desert in droves. The king of Koguryo offered to submit, and the Sui were glad of an excuse to withdraw, but the Korean ruler failed to turn up at court on the agreed date. A furious Yang-ti proposed to attack a fourth time, but the enormous cost of keeping the army in the field for so long had strained the empire beyond endurance. The emperor returned home to a country seething with rebellion. It was too late for repression, as by now

Another view of the cord and plaque style of armour, on a 7th-century figure of an infantry soldier. (British Museum)

the nobility as well as the common people were disaffected. In 617 two of his grandsons were set up as rival emperors, and in the following year Yang-ti was assassinated.

THE T'ANG, 618–907

Li Yuan, the Duke of T'ang, saw in the events of 617 an opportunity to increase his own power. He made an alliance with the Turks, who supplied him with men and horses, and moved against the Sui from his base on the northern frontier, capturing the imperial capital, Ch'ang-an. The next year, after the death of Yang-ti, he deposed the new Sui emperor and proclaimed himself founder of a successor dynasty – the T'ang. At first this was only one of perhaps a dozen rival regimes set up in different parts of China, but from the beginning the T'ang had a number of advantages over its rivals.

Li's power base in Kuan-chung in the north-west – the 'land within the passes' which had also been the cornerstone of the Ch'in and Han regimes – possessed a large and thoroughly militarised population, as well as natural defences that made it very difficult to attack from the east. The support of his northern neighbours, the T'u Ch'ueh, was also of vital importance. Furthermore, Li's enlightened treatment of Sui officials and other rivals who joined his cause, and his willingness to enrol captured enemy troops in his own armies, brought in a steady flow of willing defectors. According to the traditional account, however, the T'ang's greatest asset was Li's younger son, Li Shih-min, who is portrayed not only as the man who encouraged his indecisive father to revolt, but as a precocious military

The development of body armour, 6th-7th centuries AD: a) **Liang-tang** *or 'double armour', consisting of front and back pieces, early 6th century; b)* **Liang-tang** *with reinforcing plaques for the chest, 6th century; c and d) cord-and-plaque armour, Sui dynasty.*

genius and dashing cavalry leader who from the age of 15 led the T'ang armies to a series of stunning victories. On the evidence of the official T'ang histories, Li Shih-min is a leading candidate for the title of greatest general in Chinese history, but we must be wary of an element of bias in the records. The official accounts of this period were, after all, drawn up under the close supervision of Li Shih-min himself, after his accession to the throne.

Late in 618 a rival emperor, Hsueh Chu, defeated the T'ang and threatened Ch'ang-an. The imperial capital was saved only by Hsueh's sudden death. The next major challenge came from two warlords of the Yellow River plain, Wang Shih-ch'ung and Tou Chien-te, but after Li Shih-min's victory over Tou at Ssu-shui in 621, they surrendered. At this point a new Turkish Qaghan broke with the T'ang and invaded the north with 150,000 men, but this too was defeated. Organised opposition to the spread of T'ang power throughout China ended in 624 with the defeat of Fu Kung-shih on the lower Yangtze.

In 626 Li Shih-min forced his father to abdicate, and took the throne for himself. He ruled until 649 as Emperor T'ai-tsung, one of the most militarily successful reigns in Chinese history, and one which became a classic model for later rulers. As peace strengthened the economy and the Turks' own internal troubles reduced the threat

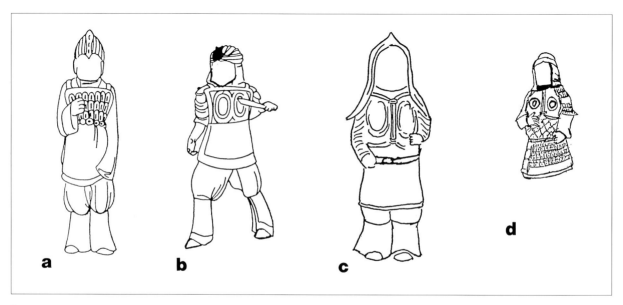

from that quarter, the T'ang began to contemplate the enlargement of the empire. In 629 the Turkish Qaghan was defeated, and 100,000 of his surrendered subjects settled on the northern frontier. In 634 the Tu-yu-hun in the far west were similarly crushed. During the 630s the cities of the Tarim Basin became Chinese vassals, and following a revolt in 644-48 the protectorate of An-hsi ('the Pacified West') was set up, with its headquarters at Kucha, to bring this area and its trade routes to the West under firmer control. Subsequently, emissaries began to arrive in China from as far afield as Sassanid Persia and Constantinople.

In 645 T'ai-tsung intervened in a dispute between his Korean vassal Silla and the old enemy, Koguryo. Despite a major victory in the field at An-shih, the T'ang failed against the frontier defences just as the Sui had, and another long drawn-out war was prevented only by T'ai-tsung's death. But the much stronger economy of the T'ang Empire was able to withstand the strain, and it continued to expand on other frontiers. The year 640 had brought the Chinese into contact with a new power in the west: Tibet. The Tibetan ruler, Srong-btsan-sgam-po, demanded a Chinese princess in marriage – implying diplomatic recognition – and after a brief invasion of Szechwan this was granted. The Tibetan empire remained China's most powerful rival until its collapse in the mid-9th century.

T'ai-tsung's successor was dominated by his consort, the Empress Wu, who is traditionally accused of ruining the empire with intrigue and extravagant spending. Nevertheless, for a time the military successes of the T'ang continued unabated. In 657 the Western Turks overran the Tarim Basin but were defeated in a great battle near Lake Issyk-kul. Their lands were divided up into Chinese protectorates that extended as far north as Lake Balkhash and as far west as Herat, so that for a few years the T'ang empire reached – in theory – more than half-way across Asia (see map). No Chinese administration was ever installed in these new lands, however, and in 665 they broke away, never to be recovered.

In 660 the T'ang once more invaded Koguryo, in alliance with Silla. The plan was to land a seaborne force in the small south-western Korean

Pottery figures of this type, representing a mounted archer, are among the most popular military subjects from the T'ang period. Note the simple bowcase, designed to carry an unstrung weapon. (British Museum)

kingdom of Paekche, then attack Koguryo simultaneously from there and from the north. Unfortunately Japanese forces became involved on the side of Paekche, inciting the people to revolt and pinning down the Chinese troops there. In 663 the T'ang navy defeated the Japanese at the battle of Kum River, enabling the two-pronged attack to go ahead, but it was another five years before Chinese and Silla forces finally took P'yong-yang and established a T'ang protectorate over Koguryo. Even then success was only temporary. In 676 a rebellion drove out the T'ang aided by Silla forces, which then proceeded to take most of Korea for themselves. One repercussion of this war was the creation in Manchuria of the P'o-hai state, which survived until it was conquered by the Khitan in the 10th century.

Meanwhile the Chinese empire had met with setbacks in Central Asia. The Tibetans had conquered the Tu-yu-hun, and in 670 they overran

Representative of another type of T'ang tomb figure, this groom's dress and features reveal his Central Asian origin. (British Museum)

the Tarim Basin. Two expeditions sent from Ch'ang-an to expel them met with disaster. In 680 Tibetan troops took the fortress of An-jung in Szechwan, which left them in control of the Szechwan and Yunnan border regions, while in the north after 682, a newly reunified Eastern Turkish state began raiding the frontier. The war in the west continued intermittently for several decades, with Tibetan invasions being either bought off or defeated in battle. The Tarim Basin was recaptured in 692, and a serious Tibetan incursion into north-west China in 700 was only repulsed after six hard-fought battles.

The war of 736-55 against Tibet saw T'ang forces once more penetrating as far west as the Pamirs. In 747 Kao Hsien-chih – a Korean general in T'ang service – outflanked the enemy by taking the provinces of Wakhan and Balur in what is now northern Pakistan. This western adventure soon brought China into conflict with the other great imperial power in Asia – the Muslim Arabs. In 751 Ferghana, nominally a vassal of the new Abbasid caliphate, asked Kao for assistance in a dispute with its neighbour, Tashkent, which was being backed by the Arabs. A Muslim force met the T'ang army at the Talas river – the only major battle ever to be fought between a Chinese and a Middle Eastern army. After an indecisive five-day struggle, Kao's Qarluq Turkish allies changed sides and Kao was forced to retreat through the White Stone Mountains. A mob of fleeing Ferghanan troops blocked the pass, and many of the trapped Chinese were captured. T'ang power in the far west was permanently broken by this defeat.

Two other major defeats occurred in 751: Nan-chao, a new power in the south-west, routed Hsien-yu Chung-t'ung's Szechwanese forces, while in the north-east a T'ang army, under the Sogdian general An Lu-shan, was lost to the Khitans, a Manchurian tribe descended from the Hsien-pi. Nan-chao established a disciplined army on Chinese lines and campaigned widely throughout south-east Asia, being at various times allied to the Tibetans and the T'ang. The war with Tibet continued until 755, when China was thrown into disarray by the rebellion of An Lu-shan, who led a mixed army of Chinese, Turks and Khitans south from his stronghold on the north-eastern frontier. Government bungling led to the loss of Ch'ang-an, and the emperor was forced to abdicate. The rebellion was not suppressed until 763, after years of fighting which devastated much of north China. In some respects the panic measures taken by the government to contain the revolt were even more damaging in the long term than the war itself. The north-western frontier was left defenceless when the garrisons were called home to protect the capital, and the decentralisation of military power which was to cripple the later T'ang was encouraged by the setting up of local military commands throughout the provinces. After peace was restored, amnestied rebel commanders of dubious reliability were given imperial offices and remained in power over much of the north-east.

Model of a pack camel, from an early-8th century tomb. (British Museum)

contented peasantry, and in the 860s bloody Nan-chao invasions of the southern province of Annam added to the dynasty's troubles. Huang Ch'ao's revolt in 874-84 marked the final stage in the decline of imperial authority. Two provincial warlords who played a vital role in suppressing Huang Ch'ao – Chu Wen and Li K'o-yung (the latter a member of the Sha-t'o Turkish tribe which had been settled within the Empire since 808) – took the opportunity to set up independent bases, from which they carried on a bitter struggle for power. The emperors were quickly reduced to mere puppets of the warlords, and the last campaign undertaken by the T'ang central government was an unsuccessful attempt to bring Li K'o-yung to heel in 890. Finally, in 907, Chu Wen deposed the T'ang emperor, slaughtered his ministers and proclaimed his own Liang dynasty. The regime which had brought China to the peak of its military prestige had come to an ignominious end.

SUI AND T'ANG ARMIES

The basis of both Sui and early T'ang armies was the *fu-ping* militia system, which had its origins in the Chinese troops conscripted by the Western Wei under Yu-wen T'ai in the 550s. The army of the Sui conquest was ethnically mixed, consisting mainly of Chinese *fu-ping* soldiers and Hsien-pi tribesmen. One modern study shows that out of 60 high-ranking officers, at least 40 per cent were non-Chinese, and 87 per cent had served under the previous dynasty – the Hsien-pi Northern Chou. The *fu-ping* was not a mass levy, but drew its manpower selectively from old hereditary military families and others charged with providing troops in lieu of liability for forced labour. Initially, military service therefore carried high social status for the families involved. These families were concentrated overwhelmingly in the north, especially in Kuan-chung, where society had already been militarised by the long series of

The series of disasters did not end there. In 763 a Tibetan army captured Ch'ang-an and installed a puppet emperor. Though he was soon driven out, the loss of the imperial horse pastures at nearby Lung-yu was more permanent.

Another spate of rebellions engulfed the north between 781 and 786, and thereafter the T'ang tended to concentrate its remaining military power in the capital, leaving the defence of the rest of the empire to provincial authorities. It is a tribute to the enormous prestige of the dynasty, however, that this did not lead at once to full-scale separatism. In fact the early-9th century saw several successful attempts to bring provinces that showed too much independence back under government control; the best known among them is the Huai-hsi campaign of 815-17.

By the 850s the general level of lawlessness and banditry was rising as the military effectiveness of the armies declined. The Che-tung rebellion of 859 was an ominous sign, since for the first time under the T'ang it involved a mass rising of dis-

wars of the previous three centuries, and where loyalty to the regime was strongest.

The *fu-ping* system continued in use under the T'ang, which maintained some 600 militia units, each containing between 800 and 1,200 men who were liable to serve between the ages of 21 and 60. While the Sui had subordinated these units to the local civil administration, the T'ang controlled them centrally, via a bureaucracy answerable to the *ping-pu* or Ministry of the Army. Units contained both cavalry and infantry, and were subdivided into *t'uan* of 200 men, *tui* of 50, and *huo* of ten. Officers were permanently employed, but the rank-and-file had to report for duty and training at the capital on a rotation system, depending upon how far away they lived. Those up to 500 *li* (about 160 miles) from the capital served one month in five; those over 2,000 *li* away, two months in every 18. A similar system provided men for three-year tours of duty in frontier garrisons. This arrangement functioned well at first because the *fu-ping* units were already concentrated on the northern frontier and in the vicinity of the capital, and it had a number of other advantages: it involved little government expenditure, since the men supported themselves for most of the year by farming; it ensured the existence of

a reserve of trained troops available for call-up in war; and it kept the army divided into small units and concentrated at the capital where it could be supervised, preventing its generals from establishing strong power bases elsewhere.

There were, however, drawbacks, which became more obvious towards the close of the 7th century. The system was only suited to the provision of guards in peacetime, or to brief campaigns by field armies (*hsing-chun*) recruited for specific operations, not to the maintenance of static defensive positions on distant frontiers, nor to protracted wars like those in Korea. If the men were kept away too long agriculture would suffer, and their clothing and weapons, which they had to supply themselves at the outset of a campaign, would become worn out. Liu Jen-kuei's report on the state of the army in Korea in 664 complains that although the men had been told to make provision for being away from home for one year, they had already been in the field for two. T'ai-tsung had tried to ensure that soldiers were rewarded for good service and their families compensated if they died, but this policy had been neglected, and consequently the men were demoralised. Well-off families began to pay substitutes or evade service altogether, and by the time of the

T'ai-tsung suggests that many were volunteers:

'When we call for ten men we get a hundred; when we call for a hundred we get a thousand.'

Others, however, were conscripted as required from ordinary non-military families. There were also regular guard units, such as the Northern Army or Army of Fathers and Sons, which was originally formed from veterans of Li Yuan's campaign against the Sui, and the *San-wei* or cadet corps, consisting of aristocratic youths undergoing training as officers. The Sui had established 12 *chun*, or standing armies, to garrison the capital in cooperation with the *fu-ping* contingents, and the T'ang retained this system, adding a number of new units.

Although much later in date, this model of a Tibetan lamellar coat gives an idea of the type of armour which was popular in Central and East Asia from the 7th century onwards. (The Board of Trustees of the Royal Armouries, no. XXVIA-18)

Empress Wu guards officers were being appointed not from *fu-ping* families but from among the relatives of court officials. The crisis in the system became obvious in 722, when the emperor planned a pilgrimage to Mount T'ai, but found that the units currently at the capital were so far below their paper strength that they could not provide an adequate escort.

From the beginning, however, T'ang armies were supplemented by troops from other sources. The 644 expedition to Korea, for example, included thousands of men from regions where the militias did not operate, and a remark attributed to

Tibetan horse armour, probably 9th-century. There are few archaeological sources for the appearance of Tibetan troops of the T'ang period, but armour styles tended to change little after the early Middle Ages. It is therefore likely that the Tibetans who fought both for and against the T'ang were equipped in very similar fashion. (The Board of Trustees of the Royal Armouries, no. XXVIA-157, 186)

*This military official, wearing a fabric **liang-tang** and a hat with characteristic bird of prey motif, comes from the tomb of Liu T'ing-hsun, who died in 728 AD. (British Museum)*

cum-agricultural colonies, where troops grew crops when not on active duty, were employed as a traditional Chinese solution to supply problems. From 737 it was decided to replace the militia entirely with paid *chien-erh* regulars; they were recruited by calling for volunteers from the population in general. However *t'uan-lien*, or emergency local militias, were still raised from time to time in areas threatened by invasion.

Both the Sui and the T'ang also relied heavily on foreign auxiliaries. T'u-ti-chi, a chief of the Mo-ho people from Manchuria, became a vassal of Sui Yang-ti and sent troops – probably mounted archers – to his aid against Koguryo. T'u-ti-chi's son was later given the rank of duke

T'ang figure in the classic pose associated with guardsmen. He appears to be wearing a long coat of lamellar armour. (British Museum)

The process of replacing the *fu-ping* system with an enlarged standing army was gradual. In the late 7th-century the frontier garrisons in remote regions began to be taken over by regular long-service troops known as *chien-erh*, many of whom were re-enlisted *fu-ping*. Then in 710 a major reform began, aiming to make the frontier forces capable of withstanding invasions without the levied expeditionary forces to support them. Nine frontier commands were established, each comprising a number of garrisons and a *ching-lueh chun*, or 'defence army', under the overall control of a governor. These men were sometimes professional soldiers, but in less seriously threatened areas court officials were preferred, since they were considered more reliable. *T'un-t'ien* military-

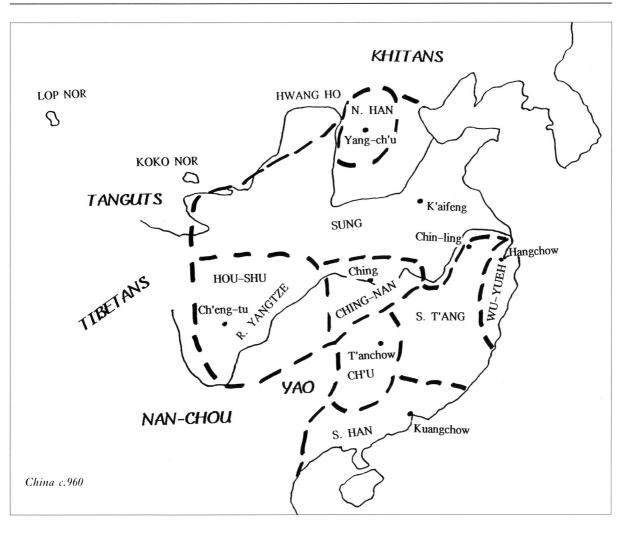

China c.960

by the T'ang for distinguished service against the Tibetans. Other Mo-ho fought for Koguryo against the T'ang in 645, but those captured by the Chinese were executed as traitors. Also prominent in Chinese service were Turks: in 605, 20,000 Eastern T'u-chueh served under Sui command against Khitan raiders, but a decade later Turkish support was instrumental in bringing the T'ang to power. T'ai-tsung attributed his success partly to the fact that whereas previous native Chinese emperors had cherished their own people at the expense of the 'barbarians', he had always valued both and treated them equally. Turks and related Central Asian cavalrymen continued to form an important part of the T'ang forces, and in the 8th century the cavalry of the allied Uighurs provided vital support to the dynasty on several occasions. Foreigners were even appointed to command armies, being thought to be more politically reliable than native Chinese – a belief which the career of An Lu-shan showed to be somewhat naïve.

After An Lu-shan's revolt, the provincial governors' forces became virtually independent private armies, often fighting among themselves. New professional units were raised by the government to counter this tendency, but they too proved difficult to control. In the 9th century the *Shen-ts'e*, or Divine Strategy army, was set up under the command of court eunuchs, and in 885 a new army 54,000 strong was established, composed largely of young men from Ch'ang-an. None of these forces was able to stand up to the battle-hardened veterans of the provincial armies. By the beginning of the 10th century, real power in the empire was held by two rival armies: that of Chu

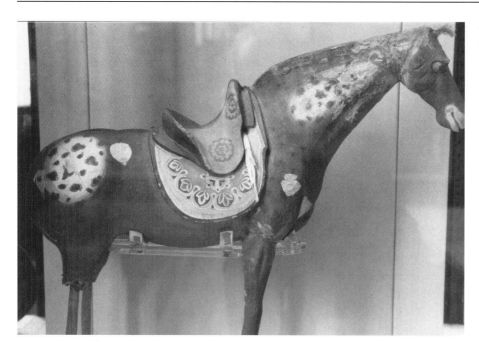

8th-century clay and wood model of a horse from Turfan, showing the typical T'ang saddle and saddle-cloth. (British Museum)

Wen, governor of Pian province, in the south, and the Sha-t'o Turks of Li K'o-yung in the north.

The Sui pioneered the system of civil service examinations, and this eventually provided China with a new ruling class, but until the end of the T'ang, high office – especially in the army – was largely the domain of aristocrats, and martial prowess was still often valued above academic training, with examinations placing emphasis on skill with the bow and lance. The career of Chang Wan-fu, a famous late-8th century general, is instructive in this respect: his father and grandfather were both scholars with official degrees, but neither rose to high rank. Chang, therefore, 'took no pleasure in books but studied horsemanship and archery ... he enlisted in the army to serve in Liao-tung and came home a general'. Youths from the old military families of the north-west trained with weapons from an early age, and the imperial family was no exception: Li Shih-min took the field in person until near the end of his life, and as late as the 780s the future emperor, Shun-tsung, took part in the wars of his father's reign, 'bow and arrows always in hand'. The T'ang ideal was *ju-hsiang, ch'u chiang* – a man who was equally accomplished at court or on campaign.

The main striking force of Sui armies was the heavy cavalry, equipped for close combat in typical 6th-century style, with lances, swords and often full armour for both men and horses. The leading military commander of the period, Yang Su, was noted for his enthusiasm for cavalry charges and aggressive tactics generally. Under the T'ang, the traditional Turkish combination of lance and bow was widely adopted even by ethnic Chinese cavalry, but probably did not replace the old-style charging cataphracts immediately. Certainly accounts of Li Shih-min's 'iron-clad' horsemen in battle are reminiscent of these earlier tactics. It seems likely, however, that the use of the very heavy cataphract equipment declined as Turkish influence spread. Some T'ang expeditionary forces in Central Asia consisted entirely of cavalry – mostly Turks or similar allies, but also including both light and heavy Chinese horse-archers – and when infantry were taken along, they were frequently mounted on horses to increase their mobility over the huge distances involved. After the upheavals of the mid-8th century, the number and effectiveness of the cavalry declined dramatically. Repeated attempts to reverse this process failed, and by the end of the 9th century, native Chinese cavalry seem to have almost disappeared. It was considered worthy of note when Chu Wen, impressed by the performance of the Sha-t'o horsemen against to throwdown their crossbows and charge, so that other men had to be sent to follow them and pick up the discarded weapons. One source gives the ratio of bows to crossbows in the ideal army as five to one. In fact this and other T'ang writings suggest that all soldiers – even those infantry who were primarily spearmen – were supposed to carry bows, but it is not clear how far this was achieved in practice.

As in earlier periods, sophisticated siege equipment was available, including artillery, towers and rams. T'ang armies on campaign protected themselves whenever possible with elaborate fortified camps. Tu Mu, a 9th-century writer, provides some interesting details on the construction of these works. Each division of the army had its own enclosed camp; these were linked together with walls and paths, and were sited 50 to 100 paces apart so that they could support each other with missiles. Small towers were built where the paths intersected, and topped with piles of firewood which could be lit as a warning of attack. Thus even if an enemy forced his way through the perimeter defences, he would find himself surrounded by smaller fortifications and illuminated by the fires, and could be shot at from raised positions on all sides. A recommended tactic was to deliberately allow an attacker to enter the complex, so that he could be trapped. Not suprisingly, Tu Mu comments that 'our only worry is that the enemy will not attack at night, for if he does he is certain to be defeated'.

Lokapala tomb guardian figure; late T'ang. It is not known whether such intricate designs were ever actually worn, but they are clearly an elaboration of the familiar cord-and-plaque construction. (British Museum)

Huang Ch'ao's rebels, raised 500 cavalry of his own.

Infantry in the 6th and 7th centuries was divided into *pu-pin*, or marching infantry, armed with spears, and *pu-she*, or archers. The crossbow, the principal weapon of Han infantry, appears to have been less common in this period than the composite bow, although there are hints that it may have retained its importance in the south.

An 11th-century writer remarks that the T'ang had so little confidence in the crossbow that they equipped its users with halberds for self defence. They then tended to succumb to the temptation

THE FIVE DYNASTIES AND TEN KINGDOMS, 907–959

This is the name traditionally given to the period of disunity between the fall of the T'ang and the Sung reunification – referring to the succession of nominally imperial dynasties established in north China, and the *de facto* independent principalities

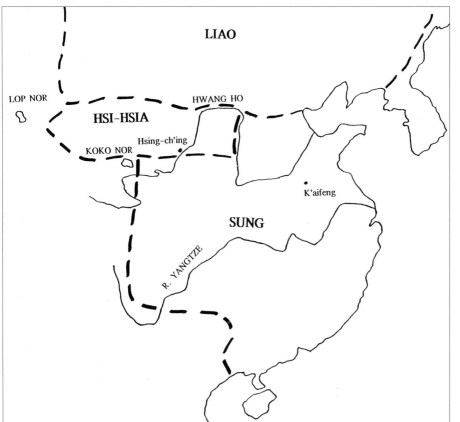

China c.1000

which divided the south among themselves. The first of the northern 'Five Dynasties' was the Later Liang established by Chu Wen; this was overthrown in 923 by the Sha-t'o Turk Li Ts'un-hsu, who claimed to be restoring T'ang imperial authority with his Later T'ang regime. Li, however, failed to provide stability, and in 936 another Sha-t'o general set up his own dynasty, the Later Chin. Meanwhile, in 907, the Khitans had established a Chinese-style dynasty – the Liao – in Manchuria, and in 943-6 fought a successful war against the Later Chin, overrunning much of north China. Faced with continuing popular resistance, the invaders withdrew, leaving the Sha-t'o commander Liu Chih-yuan with the only effective army in the region. Liu naturally lost no time in establishing himself at the head of yet another new dynasty – the Later Han. Finally, in 951, this short-lived state was replaced in a coup by one of its native Chinese officers, the founder of the Later Chou. It was this regime which was taken over in 960, after a mutiny of an army fighting

the Khitans, by a commander of the Palace Guard – Chao K'uang-yin, the first emperor of the Sung.

The forces of the Later Liang were organised into six armies, with additional units of both cavalry and infantry – apparently recruited from Chu Wen's personal followers in the civil wars at the end of the T'ang – which were based at the capital as guards. Chu's troops had originally been almost entirely infantry, but he subsequently raised several regiments of cavalry modelled on the mounted archers of the Sha-t'o Turks. The regimes which replaced the Liang were ruled by the Sha-t'o, and their military organisation reflected their Turkish ancestry, although from Li K'o-yung's time onwards many Chinese were incorporated, forming the characteristic *fan-han* mixed armies. A proportion of Chinese families – originally one in ten, but later one in seven – had each to provide one soldier, while the rest supplied food and equipment. Apart from Chinese and the Sha-t'o themselves, their forces could also include Khitans, Tatars and other Mongolian and

Turkish tribesmen. Despite their nomad ancestry, the Sha-t'o were not rich in horses, and often had to requisition them from their Chinese subjects; horses were expensive to maintain in China, and the Later T'ang dynasty is said to have spent over two-thirds of its revenue on the cavalry, even though they were still a minority of the army. It was probably to preserve scarce horses that instructions were issued that cavalry were not to be mounted while on the march, unless the enemy was sighted.

At first the Sha-t'o warriors were notoriously uncontrollable, trading on their reputation for ferocity, but in 908 Li Ts'un-hsu introduced a strict code of discipline, setting out battle dispositions and regulations for the march, and prescribing prompt execution for malingerers. He also established a Chinese-style military secretariat. The Later T'ang and Chin retained the Six Armies of the Liang – including many of their

Under the late T'ang, lamellar coats like this one, derived from Central Asian traditions, largely replaced earlier types. This well-known figure from Mingoi in the Western Regions is probably of T'ang date. Round shields were also used on occasion by T'ang cavalry. (British Museum)

Another lokapala, *this time in the famous three-colour pottery style, wears armour of similar type. (British Museum)*

native Chinese personnel – but kept a strong 'Emperor's Army' at the capital to counter any possible rebellion. The value of this was proved in 933, when the Six Armies plotted unsuccessfully to carry out a coup d'état. The Sha-t'o, who had never been very numerous, eventually disappeared by assimilation into the native Chinese population, and after 951 they ceased to play a distinct military role.

The Ten Kingdoms in the south were naturally less influenced by nomad traditions and seem to have relied largely on infantry – some of them armoured – equipped with long swords. Naval warfare was also important. The Southern Han,

Excavated from Miran on the Silk Route, these lacquered leather lamellae are among the very few surviving examples of T'ang armour. The decoration is red on black. (British Museum)

based in the far south, was notable for its ultimately unsuccessful struggle to extend its control southwards into what is now Vietnam. This regime was also unique among Chinese states in maintaining a permanent corps of elephants. The animals are said to have been crewed by ten or more men each, although in view of the maximum loads quoted for modern Indian elephants, it is

unlikely that they all actually rode in combat. The elephants were successful in battles against several local opponents, but in the Sung invasion of 970 they failed to stand up to crossbowmen, and were routed.

THE SUNG DYNASTY, 960–1279

The task of reunification upon which Chao K'uang-yin embarked in the 960s was on the face of it more formidable than that which had faced the Sui founder at the end of the last period of fragmentation. The former Chou territories which Chao took over in the north formed the strongest single political unit, but continued migration into the Yangtze valley and further south had greatly

Infantry combat, depicted on a ceramic pillow from the Northern Sung (see Plate F for a reconstruction based on this source). (British Museum)

increased the economic and manpower resources of those regions, which at that time were divided among six independent states. However, these regimes were prevented from supporting each other by mutual antagonisms. Chao cleverly took advantage of this. The small and unstable middle Yangtze states of Ching-nan and Ch'u fell first, followed by Shu in the west, which despite a popular uprising and subsequent hard fighting was under Sung control by the end of 966. In 970 the Southern Han was subdued, and five years later the Southern T'ang fell to a combined assault by the Sung and its coastal neighbour, Wu-Yueh. None of the victims had attempted to help each other, and Wu-Yueh, which had short-sightedly contributed to the Sung success, was now isolated and was forced to surrender in 978. The campaigns of conquest, now under Chao's successor Sung T'ai-tsung, were concluded in 979 by the defeat of the Northern Han, which was based in modern Shansi north-east of the Yellow River. This state was supported by the neighbouring Liao and put up strong resistance, only succumbing after a Khitan expedition was defeated by the Sung outside the city of T'ai-yuan.

However, the reunification of the empire had not been quite complete. The Khitans remained in possession of a small area around Yen-ching – the 'sixteen Yen-yun districts' – which had been part of the T'ang domains. At first T'ai-tsung attempted to recover them by force, but in 979 he suffered a decisive defeat at the Kao-liang River near Yen-ching. In 1004 the Khitans retaliated with an invasion which threatened the Sung capital at K'aifeng, but after a drawn battle at Shan-chou the two powers finally made peace. This lasted for over a century, although occasional border disputes did arise – for example in 1074, when the building of fortifications on the Sung's north-eastern frontier provoked protests from the Liao. A more lasting military threat to the Sung, however, came from the north-west.

The Tangut people – variously described as related to the Hsien-pi and the Tibetans – had maintained a presence in the Ordos steppe since at least the 9th century. In 884 one of their chiefs, Toba Ssu-kung, received from the T'ang the title of 'King of Hsia' in return for help in suppressing

Iron statue of a Sung soldier, dated 1098. (British Museum)

Huang Chou's revolt, and although the Tanguts became effectively independent after the end of the T'ang, Toba's descendants remained on good terms with China, aiding the Sung in their campaign against the Northern Han.

The Ordos region was of great strategic significance, however, both as prime grazing land for cavalry horses and because it controlled the trade routes to the west. So when civil strife broke out among the Tangut clans in the 980s, the Sung could not resist the temptation to intervene. The first of a series of seven wars lasted from 982 to 1006, and succeeded only in uniting the Tanguts in opposition to the Chinese, who for lack of cav-

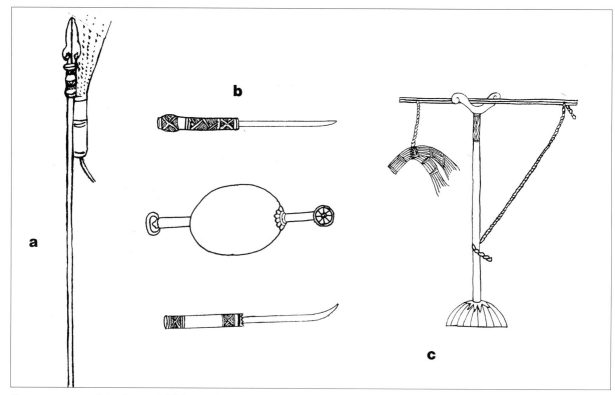

Secret weapons of the Sung: a) **Li hua ch'iang** *or 'pear-flower spear', prototype of the fire lance, from Huo Lung Ching; b) 'Thunderclap bomb' with metal brands for lighting fuses, from Wu Ching Tsung Yao; c) 'Swallowtail' incendiary device, used to lower burning material from the walls of cities onto enemy siege machinery, from Wu Ching Tsung Yao.*

alry could make little headway on the open steppes. Conflict broke out again in 1040, provoked by Chao Yuan-hao's adoption of the title of Emperor of Great Hsia, thus claiming for his Hsi-Hsia, or Western Hsia, regime equal status with its Sung overlord. Hsi-Hsia invaded the Wei Valley and inflicted heavy losses on the Chinese. The Sung won a moral victory in 1044, when Yuan-hao accepted nominal vassal status, but the truth was that the Tanguts had had to be bought off with large amounts of cash, silk and tea. The 'land within the passes', the strategic heart of previous Chinese empires, had become a devastated frontier zone.

The next clash, in 1070, was merely a bloody but indecisive border dispute, but 1081 saw another serious attempt to conquer Hsi-Hsia, which a Sung official rashly predicted would be 'as easy as breaking bamboo'. A force of 300,000 Chinese troops invaded the kingdom, in five columns. The city of Ling-chou was besieged, but the Tanguts broke the dikes which controlled the

Yellow River and flooded the Sung camp, forcing a retreat in the depths of winter. This caused enormous losses. All-out war between 1096 and 1099 was another failure for the Sung. The last Tangut war, from 1114 to 1119, was linked to the Jurchen revolt against the Liao, in which the Sung supported the former and Hsi-Hsia the latter. In 1115 the Tangut cavalry won another great victory at Tsang-ti-ho, and the Chinese effectively gave up their attempts to subjugate them.

The Sung were also trying to restore the traditional boundaries of the empire in the far south, where in 939 the Vietnamese – at least nominally under Chinese control since Han times – had established the independent kingdom of Dai Viet. An invasion in 981 was unsuccessful, and another indecisive war was fought – mainly at sea – against the Ly regime in 1073-77. Apart from brief interludes, however, the region remained permanently outside Chinese control.

The turning point in the history of the Sung came early in the 12th century, with the Jurchen

invasion. The Jurchen were a farming and cattle-raising people living north of the Khitans, and related to the Mo-ho and to the population of the former P'o-hai state. In 1114, under their chief Wan-yen Akuta, they revolted against their Liao overlords, and in the following year established their own Kin or 'Golden' dynasty. The Sung, under Emperor Hui-tsung, allied with them to attack the weakened Liao and regain the disputed 16 districts – a strategically inept decision, since the Khitan had long ago abandoned expansionist policies in China, and might have been a valuable buffer against wild tribes such as the Jurchen. The Liao dynasty was destroyed in 1125, and the Jurchen marched on into north China. K'aifeng fell and Hui-tsung was captured, forcing the government to flee south and set up a new capital at Hangchow, to which they gave the prophetic

Nomads, probably Mongols or Jurchen, from a 13th-century Sung painting, The Convoy of Wang Chao-chun. (British Museum)

name of Lin-an, or 'Temporary Peace'. Thus historians traditionally divide the dynasty into the Northern (969-1127) and Southern Sung (1127-1279), based at K'aifeng and Lin-an respectively.

The Jurchen did not stop at K'aifeng, however, but plunged on into the south, lured by the prospect of looting what was then the richest empire in the world. For a few years the Sung armies proved incapable of stopping the invaders, and the dynasty seemed doomed. While isolated units held out in parts of the north, the new emperor, Kao-tsung, was forced to take refuge with a fleet off the south coast. In this crisis it was the Sung navy which saved the day, blocking

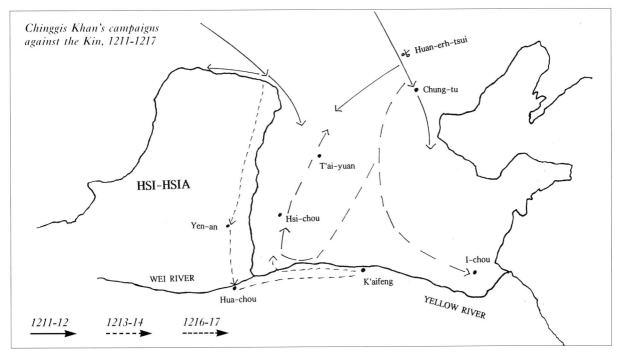

Chinggis Khan's campaigns against the Kin, 1211-1217

Huan-erh-tsui

Chung-tu

HSI-HSIA

T'ai-yuan

Yen-an

Hsi-chou

I-chou

WEI RIVER

Hua-chou

K'aifeng

YELLOW RIVER

1211-12   1213-14   1216-17

the Yangtze crossings against returning Jurchen raiders and preventing further incursions into the far south while the army rebuilt its strength. The Chinese gradually gained the initiative under the renowned general Yueh Fei, who in 1134-5 retook much of the lost territory. However, in 1141 a peace party at court persuaded the emperor to end hostilities, pay tribute to the Kin and leave them in control of the lands north of the Huai River. Yueh Fei spoke up against this and was murdered: as a result of his stand, he has been venerated ever since by patriotic Chinese.

In 1161 the Kin tried again to conquer the south, but were defeated at sea off Shantung, while a Sung river fleet prevented their land forces from crossing the Yangtze. Eventually the Jurchen troops mutinied and murdered their ruler, the bloodthirsty and widely hated usurper Hailing wang. Hostilities continued intermittently until the 1220s, with a major outbreak in 1206-8, after which the Sung were forced to pay tribute yet again. By then, however, the Kin were themselves coming under pressure from another wave of invaders from the north – the Mongols.

When Chinggis Khan's armies appeared at the rear of the Kin and began to ravage the Yellow River plain from 1209 onwards, the Sung repeated their mistake of a century before and allied with the Mongols to destroy what could have been a valuable buffer state against the new menace. In 1217 they discontinued the payment of tribute to the weakened Kin, provoking another invasion. In 1219 a Sung counterattack overran most of Shantung, and in 1222, compounding the error, the Sung general P'eng I-pin attacked Mongol-held territory in Western Shantung and Hopei. P'eng was defeated and captured in 1225 at Tsan-huang, despite a desperate attempt to stop a Mongol outflanking move by setting fire to the hillsides at his rear. Two years later another general, Li Ch'uan, was also captured, but was taken into Mongol service as governor of Shantung.

There was then a period of peace between the Mongols and the Sung, while the Mongol invaders destroyed the last remnants of the Kin, but the war resumed in 1234. By this time the Mongols, immeasurably strengthened by the newly acquired manpower of north China, were

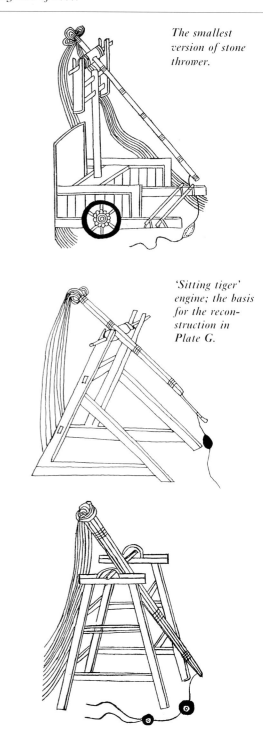

These three drawings show the different types of Sung stone-throwing engine, as illustrated in the **Wu Ching Tsung Yao** *of 1044.*

The smallest version of stone thrower.

'Sitting tiger' engine; the basis for the reconstruction in Plate G.

The largest type, the 'five pole' engine, with a throwing arm made of several pieces of bamboo lashed together.

The Sui
1: Guardsman
2: Infantryman
3: Sui or T'ang unarmoured
   infantryman

A

Cavalry of the T'ang
1: Unarmoured horse-archer
2: Armoured cavalryman

B

Elite troops of the T'ang
1: Military official
2: Imperial guardsman
3: 9th-10th-century guardsman

C

The Sha-T'o Turks
Horsemen

1

D

Hsi-Hsia king and attendants
1: King
2: Armoured cavalryman

E

The Northern Sung
1: Swordsman
2: Cavalryman

F

Sung Artillery 'Sitting Tiger' stone thrower

G

A Liao Council of War
1: Khitan Ordo cavalryman
2: General
3: Mongolian auxiliary

H

setting their sights on the conquest of the entire country. Thrown onto the defensive, the Sung were gradually encircled. In 1260 Chinggis' grandson Kubilai proclaimed himself emperor of a new dynasty – the Yuan. Within 19 years the Yuan had eclipsed the Sung and brought all China once again under one ruler (see MAA 251, *Medieval Chinese Armies, 1260-1520*).

SUNG ARMIES

Social and economic conditions in 11th-century China were very different from those which had prevailed under the T'ang. The opening up of the south had stimulated population growth, and encouraged an increase in wealth and social mobility. This has caused some to call Sung China the world's first 'modern' state. From then on an increasingly complex community could only be governed with the aid of the local scholar gentry, whose ethos was civil rather than military. Chao K'uang-yin, who feared the repetition of military coups of the kind which had brought him to power, made the best of this situation by pursuing a policy known as *chung wen ch'ing-wu*, or 'emphasising the civil and downgrading the military', and by making his generals subject to on-the-spot control by civilian overseers.

The rank-and-file were mercenaries, serving for pay and rations, and recruited from among the lower orders of society – including petty criminals, vagabonds and amnestied bandits. This was not in itself a new phenomenon, but combined with the greater rewards to be gained from commercial activity, it contributed to the low status of the military. This was to be a feature of Chinese life from the Sung onwards. In fact this *yang-ping* system, introduced in the 960s, was intended not just to supply soldiers, but as a kind of social welfare scheme, defusing popular discontent by providing employment for the destitute. However, such people were seldom loyal to the dynasty, and were despised and exploited by their officers; by the 1040s they often received only one-tenth of their promised wages. Not surprisingly, mutinies

By Sung times the synthesis of native and Central Asian traditions had produced a style of armour which was to remain unchanged for centuries. This Ming statuette of Kuan-ti, the God of War, is wearing armour very similar to that of Figure 3 in Plate C, derived from a 10th-century source. (British Museum)

were common, and deserters or 'military bandits' became a constant threat to law and order during the 11th century, especially in the north-east, where the Khitan wars had caused great hardship. In 1043, for example, the 'Winged Tigers' army defected en masse to rebels in Shantung whom they had been sent to suppress.

The *yang-ping* system proved to be extremely expensive. The population of the Northern Sung, at about 140 million, was twice that of the T'ang, and its armies were very large – 378,000 strong in 960, 900,000 in 1000, 1,259,000 by 1041. By the latter date, with government income falling, the military absorbed 80 per cent of all expenditure.

All Chinese dynasties faced difficulties due to the fact that the bulk of the armies had to be stationed near the dangerous northern and north-western frontiers, where the climate prevented the growing of sufficient food to maintain them. The Sung, however, aggravated the situation by clinging to unrealistic dreams of expansion. The wars with Hsi-Hsia, in particular, were an unnecessary luxury for a state relying on an expensive mass army which could not forage for itself in enemy territory (as, say, a mobile cavalry force might have been able to do).

Another serious weakness of the Sung military system was the shortage of horses: as in T'ang times, this was a consequence of territorial losses in the north. Furthermore, the capital at K'aifeng was very exposed to raids by the Khitan cavalry sweeping unimpeded across the Yellow River plain, and although after the beginning of the 11th century relations with the Khitans were mostly peaceful, the latter were a potential threat that could never be ignored. The peace agreement of 1004 prohibited both parties from building walls or fortifications, but the Sung often ignored this stipulation. They strongly fortified the towns which lay between K'aifeng and the border, although they did not build long walls. Cheaper and perhaps less provocative expedients used to slow down possible cavalry incursions included the ploughing of fields across the expected invasion routes and the planting of extensive barriers of willow trees.

The army had some strengths, however. Training and drill were studied scientifically, and in the best units, at least, men were allocated to different duties on the basis of examinations in shooting and various athletic pursuits. Units of *sheng-ch'uan*, or picked men, were selected for special tasks such as night assaults. Soldiers of the *chin-chun*, or palace guard, were trained in unarmed combat, and held regular boxing matches between units to maintain standards. The government was well aware of the advantages of new technology, and encouraged invention with a system of rewards.

In the reign of Emperor Shen-tsung (1068-85), the minister Wang An-shih introduced a series of reforms. He established a system of local militias, or *pao-chia*, with the dual purpose of keeping order in the districts and forming a reserve for the regular army. Each unit of ten households was to contribute a man to undergo training. In 1073 a directorate of weapons was set up to supervise armaments manufacture and improve quality. Wang also attempted to solve the horse shortage by supplying animals to peasants in suitable regions. They were allowed to use the horses for agricultural work on condition that they looked after them and compensated the government if they died. However, these reforms were opposed

Of later date, but typical of the style of fortification employed by the Sung, is this massive wall at Sian. (Duncan Head)

by conservative elements at court, and do not seem to have been fully put into effect. Certainly they did not long survive Wang's resignation in 1086.

Chang Yu, a military writer of the late Sung period, describes a system of organisation based on a squad of five, which implies that the traditional five-deep deployment was still in use. There were 50 men in a platoon, two platoons in a company, two companies in the next unit up, and so on up to an 'army' of 3,200. Chang Yu remarks: 'Each is subordinate to the superior and controls the inferior. Each is properly trained. Thus one may manage a host of a million men just as one would a few ... officers and men are ordered to advance or retreat by observing the flags and banners, and to move or stop by signals of bells and drums. Thus the valiant shall not advance alone, nor shall the coward flee.'

A wide variety of infantry weapons is illustrated in Sung manuals, including swords, spears and various types of polearm. The most important weapon, however, was the crossbow. The *Wu Ching Tsung Yao* of 1044 devotes considerable space to the crossbow – 'the strongest weapon of China, and what the four kinds of barbarian most fear'. It states that crossbowmen should be deployed in separate units and not mixed up with hand-to-hand weapons. Its readers are assured that 'when they shoot, nothing can stand in front of them', and that even an impetuous cavalry charge can be defeated by crossbows alone. Each man advanced to shoot, protecting himself with a shield, then retired to the rear of the unit to reload.

There were also crossbow specialists employed as long-range snipers: the Khitan general Hsiao T'a-lin was picked off by such a marksman at the battle of Shan-chou in 1004. Crossbows were mass-produced in state armouries, and improved designs were continually introduced, such as that presented to the emperor by Li Ting in 1068. This was made of mulberry wood and brass, and could pierce a tree at 140 paces.

Chao K'uang-yin employed tribal horse archers such as the Hsi, a Manchurian people related to the Khitans, but his successors no longer had access to the northern and western regions from which such troops were recruited. Native cavalry employed halberds, swords and even fire-lances as well as bows. Illustrations in contemporary manuals prove that armour and barding for horses was known, and at least one 10th-century painting shows what are clearly dismounted cavalry in lamellar armour – like their T'ang predecessors.

Sung armies were overwhelmingly composed of native Chinese infantry, but in the mid 13th century a number of Mongol defectors – the *T'ung-shih Chun* – were employed. According to the Yuan Official History, they 'always fought in the front rank and were ready to give their all'. They were eventually captured by Kubilai Khan who, much to their surprise, did not punish them but incorporated them into his own army. In the same period, the Sung recruited from the She tribe from south China. However these troops proved unreliable and prone to rebellion.

The development of artillery and gunpowder weapons is described in more detail below; the Sung came to rely heavily on such technology, and stone-throwers in particular were employed in very large numbers. In 979 the Emperor T'ai-tsung ordered 800 to be built, and in 1126 at least 500 machines were present at the defence of K'aifeng alone.

THE LIAO, 907–1125

The Khitans had been a significant power in Manchuria since the 5th century, and had been successful in several wars against the T'ang governors on the north-eastern frontier. It was not until 907, however, that they achieved a centralised state under Yeh-lu A-pao-chi, who set up the Liao dynasty on the Chinese model and also brought Mongolia and most of northern Manchuria under his control.

The core of the Liao army were the regular *ordo* troops, who fought as heavily armoured cavalry on armoured horses, equipped with lance, bow, sword and mace. Each soldier also provided

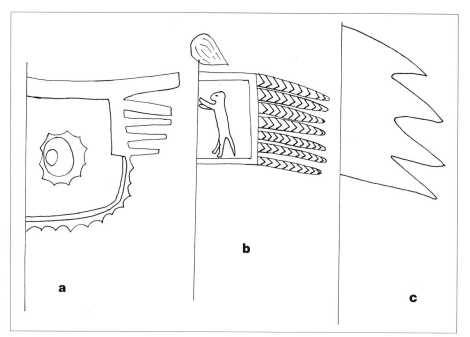

T'ang flags:
a) Carried by a mounted figure, from The Retinue of Chang I-ch'ao, Tun-huang, 9th century. Orange ground; fringe and streamers black, with white inner border below streamers; device in the centre, from the inside out, gold, blue-green, black.
b) Infantry flag from a tomb of 706 AD. Ground white, bordered red; leopard in natural colours; streamers white with black chevrons. Black horsehair on top of pole.
c) Cavalry pennon from Tun-huang.

a 'forager' and an 'orderly', and additional bows, spears and halberds (presumably used to equip these retainers in battle). The foragers were also armoured, and certainly carried weapons of some sort, and the orderlies may have done so. It is likely that this organisation translated directly into the standard battlefield deployment in three lines, with unarmoured horsemen in the first, armoured cavalry in the second, and men on armoured horses in the third. The *ordo* regulars would have provided an elite reserve in the third line, while the orderlies and foragers formed respectively an advanced skirmish line and its better equipped supports. However, there were also tribal Khitan and allied troops outside the *ordo* system, who may have fought in their traditional nomad fashion as mounted skirmishers.

The settled populations – Chinese, and men from the conquered state of P'o-hai – provided infantry levies, who were often employed on labouring duties. The P'o-hai were seldom trusted with arms, as they were bitterly opposed to Liao rule and frequently revolted. Some Chinese, however, served in formed and trained bodies, providing good-quality swordsmen, crossbowmen and artillery units. Chinese artillery was used in siege warfare, sometimes supplemented by hordes of impressed peasants, 'the old and the young', who

were forced to march ahead of the fighting troops and shield them from defenders' missiles. In this and other respects, Liao tactics foreshadowed those of the later Mongols. Both seem to have emphasised denser formations than the usual nomad horse-archer swarms.

Ordo cavalry was organised into regiments of 500 or 700 men, ten of which formed a division, with ten divisions making up an army. Attacks were carried out through a succession of controlled charges, each regiment advancing in turn before being replaced and withdrawn to rest. Banners and drums were symbols of command among the Khitans, and were no doubt used to control these manoeuvres. As soon as a unit succeeded in breaking the enemy line, the rest of the division advanced to support it.

This tactic was supposed to be repeated as often as necessary – sometimes for several days – until the enemy tired and could be broken by a concerted charge. Like many such theoretical systems, however, this would have depended on the enemy remaining passive and waiting to be attacked; it must have been very difficult to apply in practice. Certainly there were cases where Chinese opponents successfully took the initiative against the Khitans (see, for example, the Battle of Ting-hsien, below). Chinese sources also describe them as being proficient at ambushes, and at skirmishing tactics involving swift advances and retreats, another favourite ploy was to set fire to dry grass and let the wind blow the flames towards the enemy.

In 1125 the Jurchen, former vassals of the Liao, brought an 11-year rebellion to a successful conclusion and overthrew the dynasty. A Khitan remnant escaped to the west under an imperial prince, Yeh-lu Ta-shih. There they set up the Qara-Khitan regime, which defeated the Seljuk Turks and played an important role in the history of Central Asia for almost a century, until destroyed in its turn by the Mongols.

This state retained much of the Chinese culture which the Khitans had acquired, and was treated in later scholarly tradition as a bona fide Chinese dynasty – the Western Liao. However, it does not seem to have employed Chinese military technology or personnel, and it had little or no direct contact with China itself. (For further details of the Qara-Khitan see Elite 30, *Attila and the Nomad Hordes*).

Lokapala in gold-decorated armour. North China, early T'ang. (British Museum)

THE HSI HSIA, 1038–1227

During the reign of Yuan-hao (1032–48), the Hsi Hsia state is said to have deployed a total of 158,000 troops, of which 100,000 were stationed on the border with Sung China, and another 30,000 on the western frontier facing the Uighurs and Tibetans. There were also 8,000 Imperial Guards – including 3,000 heavily armoured cavalry – based in the capital, Chung-hsing. Little is known of Hsi Hsia military equipment and organisation, but their territory contained what in T'ang times had been the best horse-raising pas-

Sui or early T'ang heavy cavalryman. (British Museum)

played a major role in their defensive strategy.

On the whole the Tanguts were successful in their series of wars with the Sung, but in 1209 the Mongols began their career of world conquest with an attack on Hsi Hsia. A Tangut army commanded by Kao Liang-hui was defeated outside the town of Wu-la-hai. Another force of 70,000 men under Wei-ming Ling-kung was covering the fortress of K'ei-men, but was lured out of its defensive position and also beaten. Chinggis Khan then besieged Chung-hsing, which was saved when the defenders resorted to their usual tactic of breaking the dikes on the Yellow River. Hsi Hsia was nevertheless forced to submit, and agreed to provide troops for future Mongol campaigns. This they did against the Jurchen in 1214, but their 80,000 strong army was defeated at Lin-t'ao.

When summoned again to join the Mongols in their western campaign against the

A leather lamellar armour from Szechwan, still in use early in the 20th century. Its general appearance is typical of the early medieval period. (The Board of Trustees of the Royal Armouries, no.XXVIA-106)

tures in the empire, and they are known to have relied heavily on their cavalry; it was superior in both number and quality to that of the Sung.

Hsi Hsia armies were at first simply a collection of tribal contingents, but a Chinese-style bureaucracy was eventually set up, and the country was divided into 12 military districts under two commanding generals. Tenth-century pictures from Tun-huang show dismounted warriors wearing long, Turkish-style coats of armour and wielding bows and lances, as well as infantry equipped with fire-lances and explosive bombs. A Kin source pays tribute to the Hsi Hsia people as 'fiercely stubborn... and valiant in battle'. The country was also well provided with fortified towns, and these

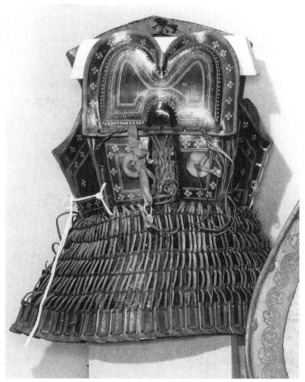

Also representative of a long tradition is this leather-laced plate armour from Yunnan in south-west China. Nan-chao infantry of the 8th-13th centuries would have virtually identical equipment. (The Board of Trustees of the Royal Armouries, no. XXVIA.161)

Khwarizmshah, the Hsi Hsia king refused. This foolish decision led to another Mongol invasion in 1227. The Tanguts were decisively defeated outside Chung-hsing – in a battle which, according to one source, took place on the frozen flood-plain of the Yellow River – and the Hsi Hsia state was extinguished.

THE KIN DYNASTY, 1125–1235

The Jurchen fought as mounted archers, and had a reputation for making good-quality armour and weapons. It appears that they were by no means as barbarous as their Chinese victims later claimed, having inherited many P'o-hai institutions and having already begun to set up a state structure even before they broke from Liao control. Wan-yen Akuta, who led the successful revolt against the Liao, died in 1123 and was succeeded by his brother Ukimai, who took the Chinese-style title of Emperor T'ai-tsung of the Kin dynasty. During the next few years the Jurchen armies overran not only that part of north China which had been occupied by the Khitan, but the whole of the Yellow River plain as far south as K'aifeng.

Unlike the Liao, the Kin abandoned early on any attempt to control the Mongolian steppes directly, preferring instead to prevent the emergence of any threat from that direction by supporting selected client chiefs, and so inciting the nomads against one another. This policy tended to inspire resentment rather than loyalty, and finally backfired when Kin support for Chinggis Khan's rivals antagonised the Khan, who united the Mongols in 1206. In 1209 a series of Mongol attacks on the Kin empire began. The state was already weakened, partly due to continual revolts by the Chinese peasantry, exacerbated by a change in the course of the notoriously unstable Yellow River in 1194, which brought catastrophic floods. At the same time the once formidable Jurchen cavalry had been neglected. The Kin were repeatedly outmanoeuvred and defeated in the field, and in 1215 their northern capital, Chung-tu, fell to the invaders. Incredibly, in 1217 Emperor Hsuan-tsung ordered an attack on the Sung, who had stopped the payment of the agreed tribute, and despite initial successes the Kin soon found themselves trapped between the Mongols in the north and the Chinese in the south. In 1235, with the fall of K'aifeng to the Mongols, the Kin empire disappeared.

Military organisation was derived from the traditional system of the tribal Jurchen, based on units called *Meng-an mou-k'o*, or 'units of a thousand and a hundred'. These were not just military formations, but social and economic units which also formed the basis of military-cum-agricultural colonies in the conquered territories. Two *p'u-nien* of 50 men each made up a *mou-k'o*, whose manpower and supplies were provided by a unit of 300 families. Ten *mou-k'o* formed a *meng-an*, or thousand. All these troops were originally mounted, and Jurchen armies of the period before their entry into China are said to have consisted entirely of cavalry. The most prestigious weapon was the bow, and Akuta himself impressed Liao ambassadors by hitting a target at the exceptional range of 320 paces. Both metal and quilted armour were known. In each *p'u-nien* 20 men were supposed to be armoured and equipped with lances or halberds, and formed the front two ranks of the standard five-deep battle formation – known as the *kuai-tzu ma*, or 'horse team'. The other three ranks consisted of lightly equipped archers. It has been suggested that this formation was designed to protect the archers from missiles while they softened up the enemy in preparation for a charge. One tradition claims that the horses of the *kuai-tzu ma* were chained together, but this unlikely tale probably reflects a habit of fighting in unusually close order, or perhaps the close co-operation between different wings of the army. The standard deployment in battle was in three bodies – a centre and two wings – and control was exercised by signalling with drums and banners.

After the conquest of the Liao Empire, Khitan, P'o-hai and Chinese troops were incorporated into the Jurchen forces, which came to rely heavily on Chinese infantry and artillery. For the campaign

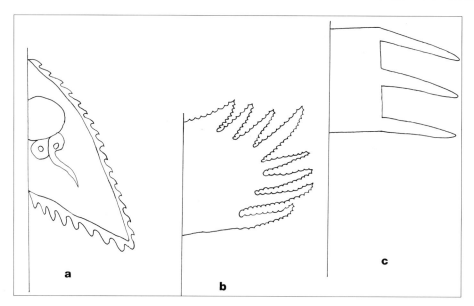

Sung and Liao flags:
a) From a 10th century Sung painting.
b) Shown on a carving of a Chinese ship from Angkor Thom, Cambodia.
c. 1185. c) Khitan, from the Wen Ch'i scroll.

of 1161, Hai-ling wang raised 120,000 Jurchen and 150,000 Chinese – the latter including 30,000 sailors. A regular Chinese infantry force, the 'Ever-Victorious Army' – which had originally been raised by the Liao – defected to the Kin from the Sung in the 1120s. Other native soldiers, the *chung-hsiao chun*, or 'loyal and filial', troops, were less well disciplined, but could nevertheless fight well. As often happened when invaders from the north established themselves in China, the cavalry eventually declined in effectiveness due to horse shortages, the difficulty of administering the traditional recruitment system under new social conditions, and the growing distaste of the aristocracy for military affairs as they began to adopt the values of the Chinese gentry. In the wars against the Mongols, therefore, the Kin relied heavily on subjects or allies like the Uighurs, Tanguts and Khitans to supply cavalry. These could be very effective, and the stubbornness of Kin resistance to the Mongols testifies to the quality of many of their troops even at this late stage: at the siege of Chung-tu, 5,000 Imperial Guards initially repulsed the Mongols, while at Ta-ch'ang-yuan in 1228, Wan-yen Ch'eng-ho-shan defeated 8,000 Mongols with just 400 cavalry and an unknown number of Chinese infantry.

Fortifications had been an important feature of Jurchen warfare since predynastic times. A favourite tactic was to block mountain passes with wooden or stone defences. After their arrival in China the Jurchen erected some impressive and technically advanced defences, including a system of long walls in Mongolia – well to the north of the present Great Wall – to control the nomad tribes. Surviving stretches show that these consisted of an outer and an inner wall, each fronted by a moat and provided with battlements, beacon towers and protruding semicircular shooting platforms known as *ma-nien* or 'horse-faces'. Cities were similarly fortified, sometimes supplemented by ingenious devices such as fields of caltrops scattered outside the walls. Chinese gunpowder weapons were also in use as early as the 1120s, and initially made a great impression on the Mongols, who quickly adopted them in their turn.

MILITARY SCIENCE AND TECHNOLOGY

In parallel with the great changes occurring in social and economic affairs, the period covered by this book saw significant advances in the military art. Of especial interest to historians is the appearance of a genre of military manuals, of which the earliest surviving is the *T'ai Pai Yin Ching* of 759. Two others from the early 11th century are also in existence: the *Hu Ch'ien Ching* of 1004, and the best known and most influential, the *Wu Ching Tsung Yao* dating from 1044. These works differed from earlier books on the art of war by including not only general tactical and strategic precepts, but detailed descriptions and illustrations of weaponry.

At the same time, interest persisted in the older tradition exemplified by works like the *Sun Tzu* and *Wu Ch'i*; influential commentators on *Sun Tzu*, for example, included Tu Mu (803–852), Mei Yao-ch'en (1002–1060) and the late Sung writer Chang Yu, who also wrote a book entitled *The Biographies of One Hundred Generals*. It was under the Sung, in fact, that the definitive list of military classics was established. Traditionally there are seven of these, attributed to periods ranging from the founding of the Chou before 1000 BC to the reign of T'ang T'ai-tsung. Most of the earlier ones, however, probably achieved roughly their present form in the Han era, and continued to undergo modification and editing until Sung scholars settled on the current versions.

It was in the field of military technology, however, that the most spectacular advances were seen. Stone-throwing artillery, based on a pivoted throwing arm powered by men pulling on ropes, had been in use as early as the Han, but it was under the Sung that it reached the peak of its development, and most of our information is derived from the manuals of that era. Three main types of machine were known. The lightest had its arm mounted on a single column support which could be fitted to a cart or wheeled base; it was therefore mobile enough to accompany the field armies, but could only shoot relatively small projectiles. The other types were fitted to triangular or semi-pyramidal four-legged bases, which were able to cope with greater stresses and so throw heavier missiles. These were often constructed on site for siege work. Although the even heavier western type of counterweighted trebuchet was not known until the 1270s, these traditional Chinese types could be quite large, with missiles of up to 130lb propelled by several hundred men

A fortified gateway at Sian. (Duncan Head)

pulling on the ropes. Effective ranges were of the order of 80 to 160 paces.

Sung manuals set out precise formulae for the construction of the different types of stone thrower, with optimum throwing arm dimensions for each weight of projectile. Range and accuracy were less than for the counterweighted type of artillery but rate of fire was considerably better, so that they were better suited to anti-personnel work – for example clearing defenders from the walls of a besieged town – than to actually battering down fortifications. A new, mobile type of artillery, with a range of 200 paces, was invented in 1176 by an officer who was being besieged by the Kin at Haichow, but it is not clear precisely how this differed from earlier models.

The defenders of towns sometimes used a rather sophisticated form of indirect fire against besiegers, with the machines themselves hidden within the walls and the fall of shot spotted by an observer in a high tower or other vantage point.

Missiles were made from stone, terracotta, metal or even ice, but at some time during the early Northern Sung they began to exploit the explosive capabilities of a new discovery – gunpowder.

Apart from simple fire-arrows, which are attested as early as the 4th century BC, the first incendiary weapon used in China was naphtha, which was introduced from the 'southern seas' – probably by the Arabs – several centuries after its first appearance in the West. 'Flying fire' was used at the siege of Yu-chang in 904, but exactly what this was is unclear; the first definite mention of a naphtha weapon is the 'fierce fire oil' which the king of Wu-Yueh offered to the Khitans in 917. This burned on contact with water and was intended mainly for naval use, being squirted onto the water in front of enemy ships by a kind of flamethrower. Wu-Yueh employed it successfully in 919 in a naval battle at Lang-shan Chiang against the rival southern state of Huai-nan, and in 975 Chu Ling-pin, an admiral of the Southern T'ang, was defeated by the Sung on the Yangtze at Chin-ling when a sudden change of wind blew his own oil back onto his fleet. Projectors were also devised to shoot the blazing liquid at the besiegers of cities. The Khitans, however, did not adopt it. They saw no reason to change their successful cavalry tactics, and their Queen Shu-lu is said to have laughed at the idea of 'attacking a country with oil'.

The first surviving mention of gunpowder in the military manuals is in the *Wu Ching Tsung Yao* of 1044, which describes soft-cased bombs thrown by artillery, but a silk banner from Tun-huang, said to originate from the middle of the 10th century, shows that primitive gunpowder devices were already in use at this date. Among the weapons illustrated in this source are a hand-hurled bomb and a fire-lance – a short barrel on the end of a pole, from which flames are emerging. This latter weapon was eventually to give rise to the hand-gun, but at this time it was no more than a close-range flame-projector, probably with an effect more moral than physical. If the date for the Tun-huang banner is correct, it must have taken a long time to become popular, since fire-lances do not start to appear in manuals and accounts of battle until the early-13th century.

They became particularly associated with the Red Jacket troops of Li Ch'uan, a Shantung warlord who fought alongside both the Sung and the Mongols.

By the 11th century the main function of explosives was as a filling for paper- or bamboo-cased bombs thrown by artillery. The formulae then used for gunpowder were relatively low in saltpetre and only semi-explosive, so that the damage caused by these projectiles was probably due mainly to incendiary rather than blast effects. Eventually this was rectified by increasing the proportion of saltpetre to around 75 per cent, and the true fragmentation bomb, enclosed in an iron casing, appeared. This weapon was known as *chien-t'ien-lei*, or 'heaven-shaking thunder', and is first described in use by the Kin at the siege of the Sung city of Ch'i-chou in 1221, although it is not known whether it was a Kin or a Sung invention. The Kin Official History describes the effects of such a bomb at the siege of K'aifeng in 1232: '. . . there was a great explosion . . . audible for more than a hundred *li* [about 30 miles] . . . When hit, even iron armour was pierced through . . . the attacking soldiers were all blown to bits, not even a trace being left behind'. Each bomb was said to affect 'more than half a *mou*' – an area of about 60 feet square. The devices could also be lowered from city walls into the besiegers' earth-works by means of iron chains.

NINE IMPORTANT BATTLES

Huo-i, 617

During Li Yuan's march from T'ai-yuan to the Sui capital, the 30,000-strong T'ang army faced a Sui force under Sung Lao-sheng. Li's sons, Li Chien-ch'eng and Li Shih-min, each commanded a wing of the army, which included 500 warriors supplied by the Turkish Qaghan. Provoked by a detachment of T'ang cavalry, Sung Lao-sheng ordered a mass charge, which was at first successful; Li Chien-ch'eng was unhorsed, and the T'ang fell back in some disarray. However, Sung's advance exposed the flank and rear of his army to the elite 'iron-clad' T'ang cavalry, under the command of Li Shih-min, who was waiting in a concealed position. He led a counter-attack which broke through into the enemy's rear, while the T'ang main body rallied and attacked them frontally. Sung Lao-sheng was captured and his army crushed.

Mount Ta-fei, 670

A T'ang army, said to be 100,000 strong, was sent under Hsieh Jen-kuei to expel the Tibetans from the Tarim Basin. Hsieh left 20,000 men with his subordinate Kuo Tai-feng on Mount Ta-fei, instructing Kuo to build two palisades to protect the baggage train, while Hsieh himself pressed on to the Chi-shih River. There he surprised and defeated a force of Tibetans, apparently not realising that this was not the enemy main body. Kuo had disobeyed the order to erect palisades, and when summoned to join Hsieh he brought the baggage with him. On the way he was attacked by 200,000 Tibetans under Mgar Khri-brin, who captured the Chinese supply train. Hsieh was forced to fall back to Mount Ta-fei, but was quickly overwhelmed by the pursuing Tibetans. Thus was the Tibetan occupation of the Tarim Basin secured.

Kao Yu, 685

The rebel leader Li Ching-yeh was defending the Hsia Ah Creek in Kiangsu against a T'ang army coming from the north under Li Hsiao-i. Five thousand imperial soldiers attempted to cross the creek in boats at night, but the defenders' best troops were waiting on the far bank and drove them off. Many were drowned. Wei Yuan-chung, a court official attached to the T'ang army to oversee the military commanders, then proposed a plan, which Li Hsiao-i adopted. As the wind was blowing from the north, the dry reeds along the creek were set on fire, and the government forces crossed while the enemy was blinded by the thick smoke. Li Ching-yeh had by this time withdrawn his elite fighters into reserve and replaced them with 'old and weary' men, who broke when the T'ang troops closed with them. The reserves were

rushed to the front line, but arrived too late to stop the rout. More than 7,000 rebels were killed in the fighting, while others were driven into the creek and drowned.

The Siege of Shih-pao, 745-749

The stronghold of Shih-pao, high in the Red Hills near the Koko Nor lake, had been held by the Tibetans since 741, and was a serious obstacle to any T'ang invasion of the Tarim Basin. Emperor Hsuan-tsung therefore ordered that it be taken at all costs. In 745 Huang-fu Wei-ming attacked the fortress, but failed and was disgraced, as was his successor, Wang Chung-ssu. Chinese armies found the conditions at this high altitude very difficult – especially in winter, when they were virtually immobilised and were forced to watch helplessly while Tibetan cavalry rode in to reinforce the garrison and harvest the grain which the besiegers had sown during the summer. T'ang losses were very heavy, and the Koko Nor region became notorious for the thousands of skeletons which lay unburied in the vicinity. Eventually command was given to a Turk in T'ang service, Qosu Khan, who in 749 launched an all-out attack with 63,000 men. After days of fighting no progress had been made, so Qosu threatened to execute his subordinate officers unless the city was taken. Desperate, they promised to do it within three days. Half the army is said to have been killed in the ensuing series of assaults, but Shih-pao finally fell within the time limit. Inside, the Chinese found a Tibetan general and a mere 400 soldiers.

T'ong Pass, 756

The rebel army of An Lu-shan, trying to reach Ch'ang-an, was halted at the T'ong Pass (site of many battles throughout Chinese history; see MAA 284 *Imperial Chinese Armies 1*, The Battle of Sha-yuan) by Qosu Khan, the victor of Shih-pao, with 180,000 T'ang troops. Other T'ang armies were closing in on the rebels from several directions, but the emperor ordered Qosu to leave his impregnable position in the pass and attack at once. The experienced general at first refused, but the emperor – advised by Qosu's rival Yang Kuo-chung – insisted. The T'ang army advanced, but was ambushed by the rebel commander Ts'ui

Ch'ien-yu in a narrow defile between the mountains and the Yellow River. With his army disintegrating Qosu fought on, trying to organise a last-ditch defence, but he was surrounded by the rebels and his own officers forced him to surrender. This unnecessary disaster allowed Ts'ui Ch'ien-yu to storm through the pass and take Ch'ang-an.

Ting-hsien, 945

A Khitan invasion of north China was opposed by the Later Chin under Fu Yen-ch'ing, who pinned the enemy by advancing in the centre with his main body of infantry, while concentrating 10,000 Sha-t'o cavalry against one flank. The Khitan army was routed, and their emperor escaped in a cart pulled by camels. This proved not to be fast enough, and he transferred ignominiously to a riding camel. Many horses and weapons were captured by the Chin.

Pei-chou, 1048

The *Mi-le-chou* rebels under Wang Tse were besieged by Sung forces in the city of Pei-chou. Dissidents within the city allowed the imperial troops inside the walls, but the rebels drove them out again. Conventional siege operations also failed disastrously: Wang's men burnt the Sung siege engines, and when the besiegers threw up a huge rampart to overlook the defences, that too was set on fire. After a month the Sung commander was replaced by a court official, Wen Yen-po, who adopted different tactics. A tunnel was dug under the city wall, and one night 200 besiegers – gagged to prevent them making any unnecessary noise – entered Pei-chou secretly by this route, overcame the guards on the walls, and let down ropes for the rest of the army to climb up. A ferocious battle raged in the streets for the next 24 hours, until superior Sung numbers began to tell. Wang Tse then released oxen with blazing tow tied to their tails, which stampeded into the government soldiers and caused panic. The rebels followed up and began to gain ground, but Wen committed special penal units which met the animals with a hail of missiles and forced them back, disordering their own side. Seeing the failure of his last ditch ploy, Wang fled.

Hsiang-yang, 1207

The frontier city of Hsiang-yang on the Han River was held for the Sung by Chao Shun. A force of Jurchen Kin cavalry blockaded it, so Chao sent out 1,000 men to drive them off, which they did successfully. However, the Kin soon returned, and on the 25th day of the siege a larger sortie was planned. Two Sung officers led more than 30 boats, carrying a total of 1,000 crossbowmen, 500 spearmen and 100 drummers, across the river to the Jurchen camp under cover of darkness. The expedition was also equipped with fire arrows and explosive 'thunderclap bombs'. Reaching the river bank beneath the enemy camp undetected, the Sung attacked with repeated volleys of missiles, supported by artillery on the city walls. The Kin horses panicked, and their army was driven off in confusion. The Sung troops then withdrew, having suffered no casualties. Later a Chinese prisoner who had escaped from the Jurchen returned to Hsiang-yang with the information that the enemy had been surprised when asleep, and had lost 2-3,000 men and 800 horses.

Huan-erh-tsui, 1211

Chinggis Khan, invading the Kin empire, was opposed by an army said to number up to 500,000 men, under Ke-shih-lieh Chih-chung. The Kin army consisted of Jurchen and Khitan cavalry as well as large numbers of Chinese infantry. Chih-chung rejected advice to strike quickly with his cavalry while the Mongols were grazing their horses after crossing the Gobi Desert, preferring instead to advance slowly so that his infantry could keep up. However, he declined to wait for a second Kin army to reinforce him.

The opposing armies met at Huan-erh-tsui, north of the passes leading to Chung-tu. Chih-chung deployed his cavalry in line in front of the infantry, but the Mongols attacked them with arrows, followed by a charge by their left wing. The Kin cavalry recoiled, colliding with their Chinese infantry and throwing both lines into confusion – 'men and horses trampling each other down in the rout and the dead being without number'. The whole army broke and was pursued through the passes, leaving the route to Chung-tu open.

THE PLATES

A: The Sui
1: Guardsman

This type of bearded, cloaked and helmeted figure is frequently found in tombs of the Sui period, and illustrates the debt owed by that dynasty to the military traditions of the 'barbarian' regimes which had ruled north China during the early part of the 6th century (see MAA 284, Imperial Chinese Armies 1). The helmet has obvious affinities with earlier leather types, and the beard suggests a non-Chinese origin. The sword is from an example in the Metropolitan Museum of Art, New York, dated to c.600 AD. The Sui Official History states that military officials carried 'lion-headed' shields, decorated in gold. These were probably similar to earlier 6th-century types with animal-head bosses (see MAA 284, Plate G). Court officials' armour could also be decorated in gold, silver or tortoise-shell.

2: Infantryman in 'cord and plaque' armour

This type of armour, distinguished by the complicated system of cords which appear to hold it together, first appears on tomb figures of the 6th century, and remains common well into the T'ang. It appears that it evolved from the earlier *liang-tang* style, in which a front and back plate were fastened together by simple straps over the shoulders. As this armour became heavier with the addition of reinforcing plates on the chest, it must have become increasingly difficult to bear the burden on these straps alone. The cords seem to be an effective means of transferring some of the weight to a yoke around the neck, and perhaps to the hips. An alternative explanation, that the function of the cords was to hold the reinforcing plaques in place, does not seem very practical. Other tomb models show that Sui cavalry wore very similar equipment, with lamellar chaps to protect the legs, and often also lamellar horse armour.

3: Sui or T'ang unarmoured infantryman

Detailed descriptions of the appearance of the rank-and-file of Sui and T'ang armies are lacking, but figures such as this – taken from a mural in an early 8th-century tomb – are probably typical of both dynasties. Each *t'uan* of 200 men was supposed to be dressed in a uniform colour, although artistic evidence does not always support this. Various colours are shown, including green, brown and white, but red was the traditional colour of soldiers' dress in China. Armament would be bows or spears – possibly both – and swords. Shields seldom appear in T'ang art, but those known from just before and after the period are very similar, suggesting that few changes took place. Most shields probably resembled that of Figure 1 in Plate F.

B: Cavalry of the T'ang
1: Unarmoured horse-archer

Based on another common type of pottery figure, this man represents one of the light cavalrymen who provided scouts and skirmishers for the T'ang armies. His long sword is typical of horsemen of the period. An 8th-century wood and clay model of a horse from Turfan has preserved details of the saddlecloth decoration.

2: Armoured cavalryman

This reconstruction is based on a relief from the tomb of T'ang T'ai-tsung, now in the Pennsylvania University Museum, showing an officer tending one of the emperor's six favourite chargers. It is therefore likely that the rider's equipment reflects that used by the emperor and his entourage on campaign. In his youth, Li Shih-min is known to have fought as a mounted archer. During the T'ang period Turkish-style coats of lamellar armour largely replaced the earlier Chinese types; leather lamellae have been excavated, often lacquered red or black, but paintings suggest that many such armours were iron.

C: Elite troops of the T'ang
1: Military official

Based on one of hundreds of such figurines excavated from T'ang tombs, this man represents an officer in formal court attire. He wears what appears to be old-fashioned *liang-tang* armour, but this was probably made of soft fabric and worn for show only.

2: Imperial guardsman
Several figurines of this type, depicting fully armoured cavalrymen in variations on the same basic colour scheme, have been recovered from the tomb of Prince Chang-huai, who was buried in 706. They clearly represent elite troops of one of the palace armies or guard units. They are not shown as carrying bows, although they may have done so on active service. The use of horse armour declined under the T'ang, and by this date it was probably restricted to use by a small elite.

3: 9th-10th-century guardsman
The source for this figure is a relief from the tomb of an emperor of the Southern T'ang, one of the T'ang's 10th-century successor states. However, long swords of this type are also known to have been used in the late-9th century, for example by Chu Wen's troops. His scale armour with shoulder pieces and waist protector is an early example of a style that was to remain popular in China until the 19th century. The colour and construction of the helmet crest are conjectural, but it closely resembles the horse decorations seen in more detail in slightly later paintings (see Plate D).

D: The Sha-T'o Turks
Based on a painted scroll from the Later T'ang dynasty, the horsemen in this procession are probably typical of the Sha-t'o aristocracy which ruled this and other northern states of the period. Their embroidered robes and head-dresses are mainly Chinese in style, though Figure D1 is dressed more traditionally. Some Sha-t'o troops, however, were uniformed; Li K'o-yung's men wore black, giving rise to the nickname 'Li's Black Crows'. Armour could have been worn underneath the outer garments.

E: Hsi-Hsia
1: King with attendants
This figure, based on an 11th-century cave paint-ing from Tun-huang, is thought to represent one of the kings of Hsi-Hsia. His embroidered robe is a typically Chinese symbol of royalty.

2: Armoured cavalryman
A 10th-century painting – also from Tun-huang – in the Musée Guimet in Paris shows several of these warriors on foot. However, the unsuitability of the armour for infantry fighting, and its similarity to the long lamellar coats used by Turkish horsemen, suggest that they are dismounted cavalry. Such armour styles are also very similar to those used in the same area by the Tibetans. The figures are shown armed with bows, but may also have used lances when mounted. A distinctive Hsi-Hsia hairstyle was imposed by Yuan Hao: the top of the head was shaved, leaving a fringe across the forehead.

F: The Northern Sung
1: Swordsman
A painted ceramic pillow of Sung date shows four infantry swordsmen and among them is this warrior in an embroidered tunic and baggy trousers. The shield is being wielded by another figure from the same source. Under Sung T'ai-tsung there were two types of shield – the *piao ch'iang* and *p'ang p'ai* – were adopted from the south.

Some infantry wore armour; paper scale armour, which was invented under the T'ang. It was made by the troops themselves and issued in large quantities. Sung soldiers were distinguished by their long hair and leather boots. If they were long-service mercenaries they may sometimes have been uniformed, but this source shows a wide variety of clothing. (For other Sung troop-types, see MAA 251, *Medieval Chinese Armies*.)

2: Cavalryman
This splendidly equipped cavalryman is based on a Northern Sung painting. His helmet and the horse's chamfron are identical to those illustrated in military manuals. The extravagant variety of polearms which was to be characteristic of later Chinese troops – both horse and foot – first began to appear in Sung times. Cavalry shields – often round – are mentioned in contemporary books, but rarely appear in art.

G: Sung artillery

A drawing in the *Wu Ching Tsung Yao* of 1044 shows this 'Sitting Tiger' stone-thrower. It is apparently so called because the triangular shape of the base reminded observers of an animal crouching ready to spring. It was powered by men pulling on ropes, and said to be the most powerful, for its size, of all the Sung engines. By the mid-11th century a primitive bomb, which made of paper with a gunpowder filling, was in widespread use.

H: A Liao Council of War
1: Khitan ordo cavalryman

The famous Wen Ch'i scroll depicts a party of these 'barbarians' in the act of looting a Chinese house. It is thought that the scroll is based on an original of the Sung period, and that the models for the figures were Khitan warriors. This man has removed his helmet, showing the soft cap worn underneath. He carries a mace as prescribed in the *Liao Shih* and illustrated in tomb paintings. Also carried were bows, spears and halberds. Jurchen, and even Mongol heavy cavalry, would have looked very similar (see Plate A, MAA 251, *Medieval Chinese Armies*).

This source shows coats in various shades of brown, and trousers as brown or blue. The Jurchen favoured bright colours such as red, yellow and white, and made much use of animal skins and furs. They arranged their hair in a pigtail and, like the later Manchus, imposed this style on their Chinese subjects as a sign of submission. Guards at the Kin court are said to have worn red or blue cuirasses, probably of lacquered leather.

2: General

This man is wearing a spectacular suit of gilded armour as depicted in the Wen Ch'i scroll, is obviously a high-ranking officer. On the scroll there are unarmoured figures shown in attendance, carrying pieces of his armour. They may therefore represent the 'orderlies' or 'foragers' who fought as lightly equipped cavalry in the Liao armies.

3: Mongolian auxiliary

A 10th-century painting shows this figure in the entourage of a Mongolian prince. He may be typical of the Mongolian tribesmen who fought for the Liao, or even of some of the Khitan themselves. He is shown as armed only with a sword, but would probably have fought in battle as a mounted archer.

FURTHER READING

The Cambridge History of China, Vol. 3: Sui and T'ang China, 589-906 (Cambridge University Press, 1979)

The Cambridge History of China, Vol. 6: Alien Regimes and Border States, 907-1368 (Cambridge University Press, 1994)

Beckwith, C., *The Tibetan Empire in Central Asia* (Princeton University Press, 1987)

Desmond Martin, H., *The Rise of Chingis Khan and his Conquest of North China* (Johns Hopkins Press, Baltimore, 1950)

Needham, J., *Science and Civilisation in China Vol. 5, Part 7: The Gunpowder Epic* (Cambridge University Press, 1989)

Pulleyblank, E., *The Background of the Rebellion of An Lu-shan* (Oxford University Press, 1955)

Ranitsch, K-H., *The Army of Tang China*, (Montvert Publications, 1995)

des Rotours, R., *Traite des Fonctionnaires et Traite de l'Armee, Traduit de la Nouvelle Histoire des T'ang* (Leiden, 1948)

Skoljar, S., *L'Artillerie de Jet a l'Epoque Sung, in Etudes Song Series 1, Vol. 2*, Sorbonne (Paris, 1971)

Tao, Jing-shen, *The Jurchen in Twelfth-Century China: A Study of Sinicization*, University of Washington (Seattle, 1976)

Wittfogel, K. and Feng, C., *History of Chinese Society-Liao 907-1125* (Macmillan, 1949)

Notes sur les planches en couleur

A : LES SUI

A1 Garde. Ce type de figure se retrouve fréquemment dans les tombes de la période Sui. Le casque présente des affinités évidentes avec les casques de cuir plus anciens et la barbe suggère une origine non-chinoise. **A2** Soldat d'infanterie en armure 'cordes et plaques'. Ce type d'armure, caractérisé par le système compliqué de cordelettes qui semble le maintenir, apparut pour la première fois sur les figures tombales au 6ème siècle et resta commun jusqu'à la période T'ang. **A3** Sui ou Soldat d'infanterie T'ang sans armure. Il est probablement typique des deux dynasties. Chaque 't'uan' de 200 hommes devait porter une couleur uniforme bien que les oeuvres d'art de l'époque ne reflètent pas toujours ceci. Le rouge était la couleur traditionnelle de l'uniforme des soldats en Chine.

B : CAVALERIE T'ANG

B1 Archer monté sans armure. Cet homme représente un des soldats de l'infanterie légère qui fournissaient des éclaireurs et tirailleurs aux armées T'ang. Sa longue épée est typique des cavaliers de l'époque. **B2** Soldat de cavalerie avec armure. Cette reconstitution s'inspire d'un bas-relief de la tombe de T'ang T'ai-tsung qui dépeint un officier en train de s'occuper de l'un des six chevaux de bataille favoris de l'Empereur. Il est donc probable que son matériel reflète celui qu'utilisaient l'Empereur et son entourage durant les campagnes.

C : TROUPES D'ELITE T'ANG.

C1 Officiel militaire. Cet homme est un officier en grande tenue de cour. Il porte ce qui semble être une armure 'liang-tang' démodée. Dans son cas cette armure était sans doute en tissu souple et portée uniquement comme vêtement cérémonial. **C2** Gardes Impériaux des troupes d'élite de l'une des Armées du Palais ou des unités de Gardes. L'utilisation du caparaçonnage pour les chevaux devint de moins en moins courante sous le T'ang et à cette époque était sans doute limitée à une élite. **C3** Garde du 9ème-10ème siècle. Son armure à écailles avec épaulettes et renforcement à la taille est un des premiers exemples d'un style qui allait rester populaire en Chine jusqu'au 19ème siècle.

D : LES TURCS SHA-T'O

Les cavaliers de cette procession sont sans doute typiques de l'aristocratie Sha-t'o qui gouvernait cet état et d'autres états du nord durant cette période. Leurs robes et leurs bandeaux brodés sont de style chinois bien que la Figure 1 porte un costume plus traditionnel. Nèanmoins, certaines troupes Sha-t'o portaient un uniforme. Les hommes de Li-K'o-yung étaient habillés de noir, ce qui leur valut le surnom de 'Corbeaux noirs de Li'. Ils portaient une armure sous leurs vêtements.

E : HSI-HSIA

H1 Roi avec sa suite. On pense que cette figure représente l'un des rois de Hsi-Hsia. Sa robe brodée est un symbole typique de la royauté chinoise. **H2** Soldats de cavalerie avec armure. Ces armures ne conviendraient pas du tout aux combats d'infanterie et elles sont très similaires aux longs manteaux lamellaires utilisés par les cavaliers turcs. On peut donc penser qu'il s'agit de soldats de cavalerie descendus de leur monture. Yuan-Hao imposa une coiffure Hsi-Hsia bien particulière : le sommet de la tête était rasé et on laissait une frange en travers du front.

F : LES SUNG DU NORD

F1 Epéiste. Certains soldats d'infanterie portaient une armure en écailles de papier, inventée sous les T'ang, fabriquée par les soldats eux-mêmes et distribuée en grandes quantités. Les soldats Sung se distinguaient par leurs cheveux longs et leurs bottes de cuir. **F2** Soldat de cavalerie. Son casque et le chanfrein du cheval sont identiques à ceux illustrés dans les manuels militaires. L'extravagante variété de trabes qui allait caractériser les troupes chinoises plus tardives (montées et à pied) commença à faire son apparition à l'époque Sung. Des boucliers de cavalerie (souvent de forme ronde) sont mentionnés dans les ouvrages contemporains mais apparaissent rarement dans les oeuvres d'art.

G : ARTILLERIE SUNG

Un dessin qui se trouve dans le 'Wu Ching Tsung Yao' de 1044 dépeint cette catapulte 'Tigre Assis', ainsi nommée, paraît-il, car la forme triangulaire de la base rappelait aux observateurs un animal tapi, prêt à bondir. Tirée par des hommes au moyen de cordes, on dit que c'était la machine la plus puissante de tout l'arsenal Sung. Vers le milieu du 11ème siècle, une bombe primitive faite de papier rempli de poudre à canon était couramment utilisée.

H : UN CONSEIL DE GUERRE LIAO

H1 Soldat de cavalerie Khitan Ordo. Cet homme a enlevé son casque et l'on peut voir le bonnet souple porté en dessous. Il porte une massue. Ils se coiffaient avec une queue de cheval et, comme les Manchus allaient le faire plus tard, imposèrent ce style à leurs sujets chinois en signe de soumission. **H2** Général. Cet homme porte une spectaculaire armure dorée. Il s'agit de toute évidence d'un officier de haut rang. **H3** Auxiliaire mongolien. Ceci est sans doute typique des tribus du Mongol qui se battirent pour le Liao ou même de certains Khitans eux-mêmes.

Farbtafeln

A: DIE SUIDYNASTIE

A1 Wachtposten. Diese Art der Figur kommt in den Gräbern aus der Suidynastie recht häufig vor. Der Helm zeigt augenfällige Ähnlichkeit mit den früheren Modellen aus Leder, und der Bart läßt auf eine nicht-chinesische Herkunft schließen. **A2** Infanterist im "Schnur- und Platten"-Panzer. Diese Art Panzer, die durch die komplizierte Anordnung von Schnüren gekennzeichnet ist, die ihn zusammenzuhalten scheinen, tauchte erstmals bei Grabfiguren aus dem 6. Jahrhundert auf, und blieb bis weit in die Tangdynastie gängig. **A3** Infanterist der Sui oder Tang ohne Rüstung. Dies war wahrscheinlich für beide Dynastien typisch. Ein jeder "tuan" aus 200 Männern sollte eigentlich in einer einheitlichen Farbe gekleidet sein, doch läßt sich dies anhand künstlerischer Darstellungen aus der Zeit nicht immer belegen. Die traditionelle Farbe der Soldatenkleidung in China war rot.

B: DIE KAVALLERIE DER TANGDYNASTIE

B1 Berittener Bogenschütze ohne Rüstung. Dieser Mann gehört der leichten Kavallerie an, die dem Heer der Tang Späher und Plänkler lieferte. Sein langes Schwert ist typisch für die Reiter dieser Zeit. **B2** Kavallerist in Rüstung. Die Quelle für diese Rekonstruktion ist ein Relief aus dem Grab von Tang Tai-tsung, das einen Offizier zeigt, der sich um eines der sechs Lieblingsschlachtrösser des Kaisers kümmert. Es läßt sich daher annehmen, daß seine Ausrüstung der des Kaisers und seiner Begleiter auf dem Feldzug ähnlich ist.

C: ELITETRUPPEN DER TANGDYNASTIE

C1 Militärbeamter. Bei diesem Mann handelt es sich um einen Offizier in formeller Hofkleidung. Er trägt eine Rüstung, die wie eine altmodische "liang-tang"-Rüstung aussieht, doch war diese wahrscheinlich aus weichem Stoff und wurde lediglich des Aussehens halber getragen. **C2** Kaiserlicher Gardist der Elitetruppe aus der Palastwachen oder Gardeeinheiten. Der Einsatz der Panzerung für Pferde ging unter der Tangdynastie zurück, und zu dieser Zeit wurde sie wahrscheinlich ausschließlich bei wenigen Elitetruppen verwendet. **C3** Gardist aus dem 9. - 10. Jahrhundert. Sein Schuppenpanzer mit Schulterstücken und Taillenschutz stellt ein frühes Beispiel für eine Machart dar, die in China bis ins 19. Jahrhundert gang und gäbe war.

D: DIE SHA-TO TÜRKEN

Die Reiter in dieser Parade sind wahrscheinlich typisch für den Adel der Sha-to, der diesen und andere nördliche Staaten dieser Zeit regierte. Ihre bestickten Roben und der Kopfschmuck sind in erster Linie chinesischen Stils, obgleich die Figur Nr. 1 traditioneller gekleidet ist. Einige Sha-to-Truppen trugen jedoch eine Uniform. Die Männer von Li Ko-yung trugen schwarz, was ihnen den Spitznamen "Lis schwarze Krähen" einbrachte. Unter den äußeren Kleidungsstücken könnte man eine Rüstung getragen haben.

E: HSI-HSIA

E1 König mit Begleitern. Man ist der Ansicht, diese Figur stelle einen der Könige der Hsi-hsia dar. Seine bestickte Robe ist ein typisch chinesisches Symbol des Königshauses. **E2** Kavallerist in Rüstung. Der Umstand, daß die Rüstung für Infanteriekämpfe gänzlich ungeeignet war und ihre Ähnlichkeit mit den langen Lamellenmänteln, die die türkischen Reiter trugen, läßt darauf schließen, daß es sich bei diesen Männern um abgesessene Kavalleristen handelt. Yuan Hao verordnete eine charakteristische Hsi-Hsia-Frisur: der Oberkopf wurde rasiert, auf der Stirn blieben Ponyfransen stehen.

F: DIE NÖRDLICHE SONGDYNASTIE

F1 Schwertträger. Einige Infanteristen trugen einen Papierschuppenpanzer, der unter der Tangdynastie erfunden wurde. Er wurde von den Truppen selbst hergestellt und war weit verbreitet. Die Songsoldaten waren durch ihr langes Haar und ihre Lederstiefel erkennbar. **F2** Kavallerist. Sein Helm und der Roßkopf am Pferd sind identisch mit denen, die in Militärhandbüchern abgebildet sind. Die überaus große Vielfalt an Streitwaffen, die für die späteren chinesischen Truppen - sowohl zu Pferd als auch zu Fuß - bezeichnend werden sollte, zeigte sich erstmals zur Zeit der Songdynastie. Kavallerieschilder, die häufig rund waren, finden in den Aufzeichnungen der damaligen Zeit zwar Erwähnung, sind aber auf künstlerischen Darstellungen kaum zu finden.

G: DIE ARTILLERIE DER SONGDYNASTIE

Eine Zeichnung im "Wu Ching Tsung Yao" aus dem Jahr 1044 zeigt diesen Steinwerfer mit dem Beinamen "Sitzender Tiger". Offenbar hieß das Gerät deswegen so, weil die dreieckige Form der Grundplatte Beobachter an ein Tier erinnerte, das sich sprungbereit hinkauert. Es wurde von Männern bedient, die an Seilen zogen und war angeblich das mächtigste Gerät seiner Größe in der ganzen Songdynastie. Mitte des 11. Jahrhunderts war eine primitive Bombe, die aus Papier und mit Schießpulver gefüllt war, bereits weit verbreitet.

H: EIN LIAO-KRIEGSRAT

H1 Kitan Ordo-Kavallerist. Dieser Mann hat seinen Helm abgenommen, wodurch die weiche Kappe, die darunter getragen wurde, sichtbar bei sich. Er hat einen Streitkolben bei sich. Die Männer trugen ihr Haar in einem Pferdeschwanz und zwangen - wie die späteren Mandschus - diese Haartracht ihren chinesischen Untertanen als Zeichen der Unterwerfung auf. **H2** General. Dieser Mann trägt eine spektakuläre, vergoldete Rüstung und ist offensichtlich ein Offizier hohen Rangs. **H3** Mongolische Hilfstruppen. Die abgebildete Figur ist unter Umständen für die mongolischen Stämme, die für die Liao kämpften, typisch, oder sogar für einige der Kitan selbst.